Crystal Reports

Formulas Explained

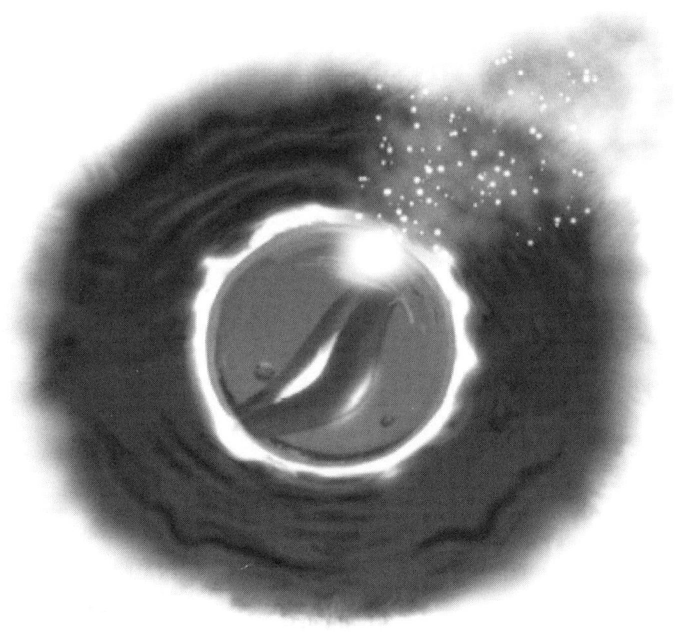

Jason Dove

Matador
5 Weir Road
Kibworth Beauchamp
Leicester LE8 0LQ, UK
Tel: (+44) 116 279 2299
Email: books@troubador.co.uk
Web: www.troubador.co.uk/matador

ISBN 978-1848762-299

A Cataloguing-in-Publication (CIP) catalogue record for this book
is available from the British Library.

Printed and bound in Great Britain by TJ International Ltd, Padstow, Cornwall.

Matador is an imprint of Troubador Publishing Ltd

Crystal Reports Formulas Explained

Jason Dove

Dedication

This book is dedicated to Zhenya, my inspiration.

About The Author

Jason Dove has worked as a Crystal Reports Consultant for over a decade, providing expertise to a wide range of industries and some of the world's largest companies.

He has worked independently as well as for Business Objects and Business Objects Partners. Jason is currently lead consultant for Scry Ltd, a consultancy specialising in high grade Business Intelligence solutions.

Accredited with CRCP and BOCP, Jason has taught Crystal Reports to all ability levels of student, both in structured classroom events and on site.

Having worked exclusively with Crystal Reports as a development tool since Version 6, Jason has used every version extensively through to the current (at the time of writing) Crystal Report 2008.

His aim in writing this book is clear:

"Throughout my entire career, one of the most common phrases I hear is: 'The software can't do it.'

"As a result, Crystal Reports has a poor reputation within the IT community, and is one of the widest implemented, yet most underutilised software packages.

"99% of the time, Crystal Reports can do 'it', or rather could do it if the Report Writer knew how to write formulas properly.

"Yet, no Crystal Reports books available cover formulas in any sort of depth….until now."

Contents

Who This Book Is For

This book is for anyone who:

- Could not quite get the results they wanted with Crystal Reports' the inbuilt Experts and Wizards.

- Has had to export a 'finished' Crystal Report into Excel to apply the additional filtering and/or formatting needed to meet the business requirements.

- Has a basic knowledge of what Crystal Report formulas can do and wants to take full advantage of the oppotunities.

This book does assume a working knowledge of Crystal Reports and does not cover the basics of report design.

Any programming knowledge or experience of Excel formulas will not hurt, but no prior coding knowledge is assumed.

Introduction: Formula Uses

So why learn how to write Crystal Reports formulas?

A formula is a piece of code written by the report writer that enables various attributes of the report to be modified. These pieces of code are saved with the report and activate every time it is refreshed.

Formulas can vary in length from a single word or number, to being hundreds of lines long.

Here are a few specific examples of the added control and features that can be added to a Crystal Report:

> Filter data beyond what is achievable using just the 'Select Expert'.
> Allow users to control report formatting.
> Apply conditional formatting to data.
> Manipulate database fields.
> Conditionally summarise data.
> Apply dynamic report headings.
> Build in security.
> Pass information to subreports.

These, and many more will be covered at length enabling you to achieve a new depth of productivity.

How to Use This Book

This book is divided into three sections.

Section One is a series of exercises which introduce a variety of uses for formulas, and how to write formula code to carry out numerous tasks.

Some of the early lessons may seem abstract, but they provide a level of understanding that will be built on later to solve more meaningful problems.

By saving each of the reports used in the Section One exercises provides a comprehensive reference library for later development work is created.

Section Two is based on one complex report created using a selection of the topics discussed in Section One and illustrates how to use formulas in conjunction with each other.

Section Three presents a collection of formulas that can be used as a reference (every one of which was originally written to meet a specific business requirement) or as an extension of the lessons from Section One.

At the very least, those new to writing Crystal Reports formulas should look over the contents of Section Three for examples of how the separate techniques taught in Section One fit together.

Experienced programmers looking for a quick overview may find all they need in Appendix A, which provides a list of the code syntax used throughout Section One. Crystal Reports has a few quirks that may trip up even seasoned programmers, and I recommend also reading through the 'Array' and 'If Statement' chapters.

SECTION ONE

Learning The Basics

How to use Section One

Section One begins with a brief overview of the Formula Editor and what is available to the developer when creating formulas. Readers with some experience of writing formulas may safely skip this.

The majority of Section One is dedicated to a series of tutorials which steadily increase in complexity as they demonstrate what formulas can do, and how they do it.

Exercises are based on real life scenarios whenever practical, to introduce how formulas can be used to resolve issues.

Completion of this section should be enough to provide the reader with sufficient knowledge to tackle most challenges that will come their way.

As well as being a comprehensive tutorial, Section One has been presented with the intention of providing an easy reference guide for future use.

The complete code for the formulas used in the lessons can be viewed in their entirety in Appendix A: Code Listings.

The Formula Editor

Irrespective of a formula's purpose, whether it is for record selection or formatting an address, they are created within the Formula Editor using the same commands and functions. The only difference is the output. The more experienced a report writer becomes, the greater the percentage of their time is spent in the Formula Editor.

The Formula Editor can be accessed via:

- The icon which is next to most of the properties within Crystal Reports.

- The Record Selection option on the Report Menu.

- Creating a new formula through the Field Explorer.

The Formula Editor

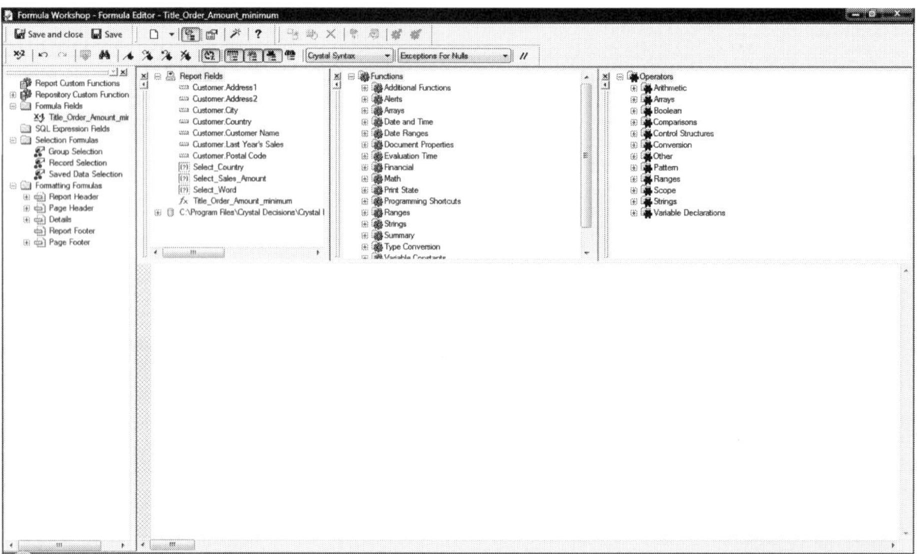

Fields, functions and operators occupy the top three panels. Their contents can be added to the bottom panel (the 'working area') by double clicking on a particular item.

By the nature of this setup, it is possible to browse for the items you may wish to use in a formula without having to memorise them all. Just having a rough idea of what is available and how formulas fit together is enough to open a lot of possible solutions to reporting problems.

If you need further information on a particular function, highlight the function in question, and click on the Help Icon (?). The relevant help page will open automatically. The help in Crystal Reports for functions is very comprehensive and in most cases provides examples to clarify their usage.

The left panel lists all the formulas within the report and provides access to any formula in the Crystal Repository if Crystal Enterprise / Business Objects is being used to store user created functions (this is not present in some earlier versions of Crystal Reports).

Crystal Reports will allow a badly written formula to be saved but will display a warning message first:

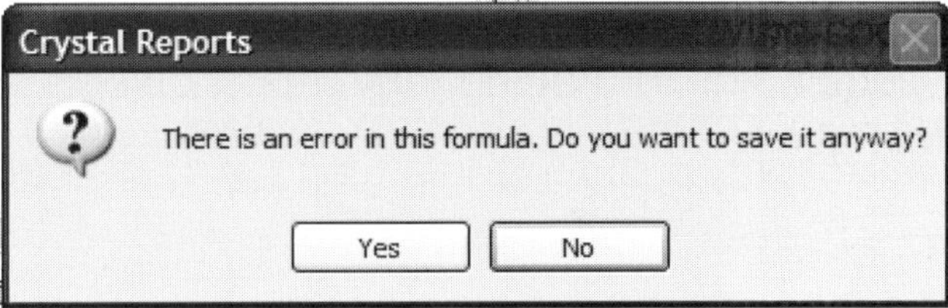

A formula can be checked for correct syntax at any time by clicking the $x \cdot 2$ icon.

NB: it is nearly always a bad idea to save a formula which contains an error.

There are three things to remember with the syntax checking:

1. Many longer formulas, when checked, will not pass until they are completed.

2. The check only looks at the syntax - a formula may still not return the correct result even If it passes the check. Think of the syntax check as a spell check, but the grammar has to be correct to get the proper meaning.

3. A formula may be syntactically correct but may not cater for certain values that may appear in the database and this will not be apparent until the report is refreshed.

Once complete, save the formula using either the 'Save' icon or the 'Save and Close' icon.

The formula will be automatically checked before saving.

The formula is automatically placed in the Field Explorer for inclusion in the report (either directly or for use in another formula), or in the case of conditional formatting and Record Selection, it will be assigned directly.

When used for conditional formatting, any report objects which have an active formula will display a red formula Icon ( ) instead of the usual blue icon ( ).

A formula that has been 'commented out' will cause the Icon to change back to blue.

Component Parts

Formulas are comprised of one or more of the following, which can be combined to meet a variety of means:

> Operators
> Literal Values
> Database Fields
> Keywords
> Functions
> Comments
> Variables

Operators

Operators are not only mathematical, such as "+", "-", "*" etc, but also include certain programming constructs like the If Statement and arrays.

NB: Unlike many other programming languages Crystal Reports uses '=' only to compare different values and ':=' to assign values.

Example (Assuming x is equal to 2, and y is equal to 3):

$$x = y + 5$$

Will compare x to y + 5 and return False.

$$x := y + 5$$

Will set x to 8 (ie the 3 from y plus the 5).

This is a common cause of a lot formula errors and is something to watch out for, and will be covered in detail later.

Literal Values

Which are just that, values which you type directly into the formula.

Different syntax is used depending on the type of value added:

Literal Vale	Type Of Syntax
Number	999 or 999.99
Text / String / Characters	"Text in here" or 'in here' (NB: first one is preferred as ' can appear within normal text)
Date	#01 01 2010#
Date Time	#01 01 2010 00 00 00#
Boolean	True or False (NB: no speech marks)

While it is very unlikely you will ever use a literal on its own, they are very handy for comparing values in function results or database fields.

Database Fields

Database fields or any other type of data that Crystal Reports imports from an external data source (including spreadsheets, text documents, OLAP Cubes) are all treated the same once 'inside' the Formula Editor and provide the basis of the report and also usually the basis of all the formulas.

Database fields are displayed surrounded by { }.

Keywords

Words that already have a specific purpose within Crystal Reports and so cannot be used for anything else.

Keywords change color when typed so they are pretty obvious. Here are some examples:

Currentdate
Pagenumber
Recordnumber
If
While

Because text values have to be surrounded by speech marks anyway, keywords are not a problem with literal values, but can cause problems when used as variable names.

Variables

Variables are like temporary database fields which are created within formulas to hold values while you manipulate them. Variables have data types, just like database fields which must be specified when a variable is defined.

Variables also have a scope. The scope defines where the variable can be used / seen within the report.

Crystal Reports has three types of scope option:

Scope Type	Visibility
Local	The variable and its' contents can only be seen within the formula where it is created
Global	The default is Global if none is specified by the user. Can be seen, used, and updated anywhere within the report.
Shared	A variable defined in a report which can be seen in a subreport.

Functions

Functions are pre-written formulas, which can be included in any formula you write to perform specific tasks. Over the years and releases, Crystal Reports has built a comprehensive catalogue of functions to cover all the most common requirements.

From Crystal Reports version 10 it is possible to create your own functions and add them into the Crystal Enterprise Repository for use by other developers.

The main body of Section One will focus on the correct usage of functions.

You will never be expected to learn them all, but having an idea of what is available can go a long way to reducing report writing time.

Comments

Comments do not carry out any practical purpose in a formula and are not used by Crystal Reports. When writing a particularly complex formula it is considered good practise to include comments to explain what or why something is happening. This is useful for other developers who may need to amend your work at a later date, or for yourself if returning to work months after its initial creation.

For Crystal Reports to ignore any text in a formula, type in "//". Anything typed after that, on the same line, will turn green and be ignored.

This can be useful for 'commenting out' lines of a formula that you may wish to replace but aren't confident enough to delete them straight away.

Naming Conventions

I recommend the adoption of a meaningful and consistent naming convention for formulas, variables and any other component that can be named by the report writer.

The actual style of the convention chosen is at your own discretion, consistency of use is the more important.

For the basis of this book I shall be using the following structure:

Begin each new word within a name with an upper case letter and use a prefix to denote the type of component or variable it is.

Prefixes:

frm	Formulas.
prm	Parameters.
rtl	Running Totals.
str	String Variables.
int	Number Variables.
bln	Boolean Variables.
cur	Currency Variables.
dte	Date Variables.
dtm	Date Time Variables.
tme	Time Variables.
a	Prefixed before the variable prefixes to denote an array of that type.
r	Prefixed before the variable prefixes to denote a Range of that type.

An array variable of customer surnames will be:

astrCustomerSurname

A range of employee holiday dates is:

rdteEmployeeHoliday

During exercises I will only suggest a specific name for a formula / parameter / running total if it is to be referenced again.

NB: While abbreviations are permissible, they are seldom consistent and should be avoided If possible.

Formula Facts and General Tips

Common Shortcuts

The Formula Editor responds to a lot of the same commands as word processing software, as well as some extra ones.

Right click in the lower panel for a context sensitive menu that enables Cut, Copy and Paste.

The usual Windows conventions also work:

CTRL A   Select everything (not available via the right click menu).
CTRL C   Copy selected text.
CTRL X   Cut selected text.
CTRL V   Paste text previously copied or cut.
CTRL F   Opens the Find Window (not available via the right click menu in some versions of Crystal Reports).

The Find Window is worth an extra mention. While it does vary depending on release, Crystal Reports XI onwards not only allows a particular piece of text to be searched for within the current formula, but also across all formula within the report.

This function can also be used to replace a particular piece of text in the current formula, but each formula must be altered individually.

Text can be highlighted and drag/dropped to new locations. By holding down CTRL whilst moving text, a copy of the text will be made at the new location but the original will be left in place.

Bookmarks

The Bookmark icons are denoted by the blue flag. These have no impact on how the formula will behave when run, but act as markers in the left margin for particular lines of code.

When writing larger formulas this is a very handy tool.

The plain blue flag adds a bookmark to the line of the formula where the cursor is when it is clicked. If a bookmark is already present, this action will remove it.

The icons with the blue flag and an arrow are used move between bookmarks.

The blue flag and cross, deletes all the bookmarks in the formula.

NB: Bookmarks are not saved with the formula, they are only for reference while coding and are lost when the formula is closed.

Formulas in use by The Report

Any standalone formula displayed in the Field Explorer will have a green tick if it is in use anywhere in the report. This includes if it is in use in another formula or chart as well as being physically placed in the report itself.

Any attempt to delete a formula that is in use will either prompt a warning message before deleting, or not allow deletion at all depending on the version.

NB: If a formula populates a variable which is used by another formula, it will not be 'ticked' or counted as being in use so will be deleted without warning.

Training Database Setup

The following selection of tutorials is based on the Xtreme Microsoft Access Database which is shipped with most versions of Crystal Reports and can be found in the '\Samples\En\Databases\' directory.

NB: Depending on which options were selected during the installation of Crystal Reports, Xtreme may need to be installed separately. To do this, insert the Crystal Reports installation disk and select the appropriate options, or download it separately if Crystal Reports was purchased as an electronic copy only.

Before commencing with the exercises it is recommended that a link to the database is created and saved to Favourites folder for ease of reference later.

Each exercise begins with a table listing the required basic set up for a report in order to successfully complete the task. In most cases the basic setup is the same or very similar for numerous exercises, so for those working through them in order there is no need to create a new report every time.

Whenever possible, practical examples are used as a basis for the lessons.

In some cases this is not possible due to the limited scope of the Xtreme content, so the student is recommended to focus on the 'how' rather than the 'why' with some of the following exercises.

String Manipulation

Basic Strings

A String is a type of database field which consists of one or more characters of text, including numeric characters.

String fields consisting purely of numbers cannot be summarised by Sum or Average.

Both single and double quotes will work within Crystal Reports. However, it is worth checking which is compatible with the database you are reporting on.

NB: Whenever possible, use double quotes as single quotes are sometimes used within String fields, especially name fields.

Using Strings

Report Name: String_uses.rpt

Report Requirement: Examining the properties of string fields.

Report Details:

Table(s)	Fields
Employee	Last Name First Name Home Phone SSN

The first step in this very simple report is to add the text "Employee Full Name: " in the Detail Section to the left of the database fields.

1. Create a new formula (Right click on 'Formula Fields', and select 'New') called "frmFullName".

2. Enter the following into the formula:

> "Employee Full Name:"

3. Save the formula.

4. Place the formula in the Details Section.

5. Preview the report.

The text entered in the formula appears in each line of the report.

Joining (Concatenating) Strings Together

The next step is to add the two name fields to the formula so they can be consistently formatted.

6. Open the formula "frmFullName" for editing (Highlight the formula then right click, and select 'Edit').

7. Amend the existing code to add the First Name. Do this by typing the '&' then locating the field 'First Name' in the top left panel:

> "Employee Full Name: " & {Employee.First Name}

The '&' character joins separate strings together, whether they are text in the formula or a database field.

8. Add the following code to the existing code (NB: the space between the " ", this is to add a space between the two parts of the name:

> & " " & {Employee.Last Name}

The final code should look like this:

"Employee Full Name: " & {Employee.First Name} & " " & {Employee.Last Name};

9. Save the changes to the formula.

10. Preview the report and resize the formula to accommodate the increase in text.

NB: It is possible, and quite common, to base groups on formula that concatenate two or more fields together.

Another common use for this type of formula is to create meaningful titles for a report and can include more than just strings.

11. Create a formula "frmReportTitle" and enter the following code (NB: PrintDate is found in the Functions Panel under 'Document Properties'):

"List Of Employees" & CHRW(13) & "Report Run: " & PrintDate;

12. Save and close the formula, then add it to the Report Header Section.

13. Preview the report.

The formula will need resizing because the "CHRW(13)" part of the formula is a 'return' that add a new line.

NB: A quicker way to create the above examples is to type the required string into a textbox, then drag and drop the fields in. However, when creating more complicated titles or headings this is not an option as discussed in the later Chapter **Parameter Based Report Titles**.

Using Common String Functions

Crystal Reports comes with an extensive collection of functions specifically for manipulating strings, all of which are accessible from the Strings Directory in the Functions Panel.

To illustrate some of the more commonly used functions we are going to create a formula to remove the bracketed code at the front of the Home Phone Field and replace the '-' that separates the phone number with a space.

NB: The Home Phone is a string field as is often the case with telephone numbers, which need to hold leading zeros which would vanish in a number field.

First, the bracketed code is to be removed. Because the length of the code is known to be 5 characters long, the formula can be coded to retain everything from the sixth character onwards.

But for the sake of this exercise, the formula will search for the ')' as if the length of the code may vary.

14. Create a new formula called "frmRemoveCode" and enter the following code to identify the position after the ')' character:

```
InStr({Employee.Home Phone},")") + 1;
```

15. Save and close the formula.

16. Add the formula into the Details Section to the right of the Home Phone field and preview the report.

The formula identifies the first position within the string that matches. Even if the number of digits within the brackets were to change, the formula would still work.

The next step is to use this number to determine how much of the Home Phone field to retain.

    17. Open the "frmRemoveCode" formula and add the following in front of the existing code:

        Mid({Employee.Home Phone},

      Complete the formula with a right bracket:

        Mid({Employee.Home Phone},InStr({Employee.Home Phone},")") + 1);

    18. Save and close the formula.

    19. Preview the report. The formula may need resizing.

The final stage, is to replace the '-' with a space.

    20. Open the frmRemoveCode formula and add the following in front of the existing code:

        Replace(

      End the formula with:

        ),"-"," ");

The final formula should match the following:

        Replace(Mid({Employee.Home Phone},InStr({Employee.Home Phone},")") + 1),"-"," ")

    21. Save and close the formula and preview the report.

The final requirement for this report is to display the last five characters of the SSN field.

22. Create a new formula called "frmLastFive" and enter the following code to select the last five characters:

    Right({Employee.SSN},5);

23. Save and close the formula.

24. Add the formula into the Details Section and preview the report.

As well as the Right Function, a Left Function also exists for extracting the characters from the beginning of a string.

If extracting a number of characters from the start or end of a string, use Left or Right respectively.

However, use Mid to extract a number of characters from within a string (ie 'Mid' String).

NB: The Mid Function can be used with an additional number to limit the number of characters extracted. For example, in case of the previous exercise, if only three characters were to be displayed after the right bracket:

Mid({Employee.Home Phone},InStr({Employee.Home Phone},")") + 1,3)

Two other helpful functions are Len and ReplicateString.

To illustrate their use, the frmFullName formula is going to be modified so that it aligns to both the left and right.

25. Open the formula frmFullName for editing (Highlight the formula then right click, and select 'Edit').

26. After ""Employee Full Name:" &" insert the following to copy the underscore twenty times between the heading and the Employee Name:

ReplicateString("_",20

Add the following code to find the length of the Employee Name and subtract it from twenty:

-Len({Employee.First Name} & {Employee.Last Name})) &

The full formula should look like this:

```
"Employee Full Name:" &
ReplicateString ("_",20 - Len( {Employee.First Name} &
{Employee.Last Name})) & {Employee.First Name} &
" " & {Employee.Last Name};
```

27. A final step is needed in order for the formula to be displayed as required. Format the 'Character Spacing Exactly:' to 4 (assuming the Font size is 8 Arial, if not, some tweaking maybe required).

28. Save and close the formula.

29. Preview the report.

The formula displays the Employee Name spaced out evenly by using the length of the string to judge how many underscores to display.

Case Manipulation

Three functions which are handy for formatting text are:

UpperCase
LowerCase
ProperCase

30. Create a new formula called "frmDifferentCase".

31. Enter the following code to build a string:

> "EMPLOYEE FULL NAME: " & {Employee.First Name} &
> " " & {Employee.Last Name}

32. Save and close the formula and add it into the Details Section, and preview the report.

The formula is very similar to the original version of "frmFullName", with the exception of the title being upper case.

33. Open the formula "frmDifferentCase" for editing (Highlight the formula then right click, and select 'Edit').

34. After ""Employee Full Name:" &" insert the following to copy the underscore twenty times between the heading and the Employee Name:

> ProperCase("EMPLOYEE FULL NAME: ") &
> UpperCase({Employee.First Name}) & " " &
> LowerCase({Employee.Last Name});

35. Save and close the formula and preview the report.

The formula is displayed in such a way as to make it clear how these particular functions impact on text.

These functions can be of great help when converting strings from databases.

In particular, if a database is set to "Case Sensitive", when running a report, any parameters or filters must be in the same case as the data in order to return a row successfully.

These functions can be used to change the case of user entered values to ensure they match and/or change the case of the data returned (ProperCase is particularly useful for this).

Extra Options for String Manipulation

A string is called a string because it is a string of characters. And each of these characters can be identified by an index number.

This is covered in greater depth later. However, this is a commonly used alternative to the Mid Function, so a brief list of examples are provided here.

To identify a character or characters in a string, place the index number of that character in square brackets after the field.

Displays the first character:

{Employee.Last Name} [1]

Displays the first six characters:

{Employee.Last Name} [1 to 6]

Displays the last character, after using the Len Function to identify the last character in the string:

{Employee.Last Name} [Len({Employee.Last Name})]

Numeric Calculations and Summaries

The most common reason for creating a Crystal Report is to summarise and manipulate data. The standard summary operations provide a wide variety of means to achieve this but these can be greatly extended with the use of formulas.

Mathematical Possibilities

In addition to the standard collection of mathematical symbols available in the Arithmetic Folder in the Operators Panel, a quick look through the Math and Financial folders in the Functions panel will reveal an extensive list of possibilities for creating math based formula.

Like all functions, mathematical functions can be nested and referenced in order to build more complex formula as required.

Report Name: Maths_Examples.rpt

Report Requirement: Examples of using maths functions.

Report Details:

Table(s)	Fields
Orders_Detail	Order ID Unit Price Quantity

The first addition to this report is to display the VAT amount of 17.5% for each Unit Price.

1. Create a new formula called "frmVAT".

2. Enter the following code to calculate the percent per Unit:

    {Orders_Detail.Unit Price} * 0.175;

3. Save and close the formula.

4.   Insert the formula into the Detail Section.

5. Preview the report.

The next addition to this report is to add the VAT amount of 17.5% to each Unit Price.

6. Create a new formula called "frmWithVAT".

7. Enter the following code to calculate the percent per Unit:

```
{Orders_Detail.Unit Price} + ({Orders_Detail.Unit Price} *
0.175);
```

8. Save and close the formula.

9. Insert the formula into the Detail Section.

10. Preview the report.

The final addition to Detail Section is to generate the total Unit Price taking into account the amount ordered.

11. Create a new formula called "frmLineTotalVAT".

12. Enter the following code to calculate the percent per Unit:

```
({Orders_Detail.Unit Price} + ({Orders_Detail.Unit Price} *
0.175)) * {Orders_Detail.Quantity}
```

13. Save and close the formula.

14. Insert the formula into the Detail Section and preview the report.

With all the VAT amended values displayed, the only remaining thing to do is add the standard summaries.

15. Right click on frmLineTotalVAT and select Insert, summary in the same manner used on normal database fields, and add a Sum based on the Group Order ID.

16. Preview the report.

Once the summaries are generated in a report, they can also be used within another formula for further manipulation.

To demonstrate this, the next exercise calculates the average price per Unit including VAT and the quantity ordered.

17. Add a Sum Summary based on the Order ID Group for the Quantity Field.

18. Create a new formula called "frmAverageUnitCost".

19. Enter the following code (NB: add the Sum functions by locating them in the Report Field Panel and double clicking them, in the same manner as for any database field):

    Sum ({@frmLineTotalVAT}, {Orders_Detail.Order ID}) / Sum ({Orders_Detail.Quantity}, {Orders_Detail.Order ID});

20. Save and close the formula.

21. Insert the formula into the Group Footer Section.

22. Preview the report.

The average value for each Unit including VAT is now displayed.

This total is created based on the summary of a formula (which is based on a database field) divided by a summarised database field.

Creating Summaries in Formulas

The previous exercise illustrates another convenient and powerful feature of formulas - namely, that summary operations can be created on the fly directly within code.

Unlike the example above, the summary does not have to exist already. The only proviso being that if the summary is to be based on a group, that group must exist within the report.

Writing a summary operation by hand may seem long winded at first, but with practice it can save a lot of time (compared to closing the formula you are working on, creating a summary, re-opening the formula and selecting the summary for inclusion).

It is easy to see how summary functions are created if we look at one of the summaries used in the "frmAverageUnitCost" formula:

Sum ({Orders_Detail.Quantity}, {Orders_Detail.Order ID})

The first part of the function is the summary operation, the second part is the field to be summarised, and the third is the field the summary is based on.

By removing the field after the comma (the field the summary is grouped on) a grand total is created:

Sum ({Orders_Detail.Quantity})

Date groups need a fourth option to state the unit of time the summary is based on.

To illustrate this, a formula to display the average Unit Price before VAT (not taking into account to amount ordered).

23. Create a formula called "frmAverageBeforeVAT".

24. First, create a Sum for the Unit Price, which is grouped by the Order ID:

> Sum({Orders_Detail.Unit Price}, {Orders_Detail.Order ID})

Divide this by the number of different Products:

> / Count({Orders_Detail.Product ID}, {Orders_Detail.Order ID})

The whole formula should look like this:

> Sum({Orders_Detail.Unit Price}, {Orders_Detail.Order ID}) / Count({Orders_Detail.Product ID}, {Orders_Detail.Order ID});

25. Save and close the formula, then insert it into the Group Footer.

26. Preview the report.

The frmAverageBeforeVAT now shows the average price of the different products within an order.

When creating a summary on a numeric field, the Summary Window provides a tick box to "Show as a percentage of", which is a quick way to display a summary as percentage of its own total.

To create a percentage based on comparisons against other fields, a formula must be employed to manually create the calculation.

Report Name: Percentage_Example.rpt

Report Requirement: In the case of this exercise, the requirement is to display the percentage of orders which were shipped before the required date per Customer.

Report Details:

Table(s)	Fields
Orders	Order ID Required Date Ship Date Customer ID

1. Create the formula "frmOnTime", and add the following code:

    ```
    If {Orders.Ship Date} < {Orders.Required Date} Then
            1
    Else
            0;
    ```

2. Insert a Group Sum Summary for frmOnTime.

3. Insert a Group Count Summary for Order ID.

4. Create the formula "frmPercentOntime" and add the following code:

    ```
    (Sum({@frmOnTime}, {Orders.Customer ID})
    /
    Count({Orders.Order ID}, {Orders.Customer ID})) * 100;
    ```

5. Save and close the formula, and insert it into the Group Footer Section.

6. Preview the report.

The percentage of orders shipped before their required date is now displayed per customer.

Creating an overall percent for the entire report is a straight forward task:

7. Create the formula "frmPercentOverall" and add the following code:

```
(Sum({@frmOnTime})
/
Count({Orders.Order ID}) * 100;
```

8. Save and close the formula, and insert it into the Report Footer Section.

9. Preview the report.

NB: In the same way as a summary can be placed in either a Header or Footer Section, the same applies to a formula which carries out the same functions.

Always Round Up

One mathematical rule which is often overlooked is that if the digit being 'rounded' is a 5, whether it is rounded up or down is dictated by whether the number to its left is odd or even.

 This particular rule is adhered to by some software and not others (and sometimes varies between versions of the same software).

NB: This particular exercise does not use any database fields. This is to enable different values to be evaluated and easily test all possible outcomes.

10. Create a new formula called "frmAlwaysRoundUp".

11. Enter the following code:

```
Round(3.5,0);
```

12. Save and close the formula.

13. Insert the formula into the Report Header Section and preview the report.

The formula will evaluate to '4'.

14. Open the formula called "frmAlwaysRoundUp".

15. Replace the existing code the following:

> Round(4.5,0);

16. Save and close the formula and preview the report.

The formula should still equate to '4', however, it actually rounds up to 5.

17. Open the formula called "frmAlwaysRoundUp".

18. Replace the existing code the following, a variable to hold the various numbers we are going to round:

> numberVar intNumber := 5.5;

The first condition of the If Statement (see **Using If Statements** for a full explanation) checks to see if intNumber ends in 5, if it doesn't the normal Round Function can be used:

> If (Truncate(intNumber,0) + 0.5) <> intNumber Then
>   Round(intNumber)

The Remainder is used to check if intNumber is odd, if it is, the RoundUp Function is used:

> Else If Remainder(Truncate(intNumber,0),2) > 0 Then
>   RoundUp(intNumber)

If intNumber is not odd, it must be even, to the last option rounds down using the Truncate Function:

```
    Else
            Truncate(intNumber,0);
```

The final formula should look like this:

```
numberVar intNumber := 5.5;

If (Truncate(intNumber,0) + 0.5) <> intNumber Then
        Round(intNumber)
Else If Remainder(Truncate(intNumber,0),2) > 0 Then
        RoundUp(intNumber)
Else
        Truncate(intNumber,0);
```

19. Save and close the formula, then preview the report.

Because intNumber is 5.5, the formula will display a '6'.

NB: There is no 'RoundDown' Function in Crystal Reports because this requirement is handled by the Truncate Function.

To fully test the formula, amend the first line of frmAlwaysRoundUp to each of these values in turn, and preview the report for each one:

```
numberVar intNumber := 4.5;

numberVar intNumber := 8.3;

numberVar intNumber := 10.8;

numberVar intNumber := 6.0;
```

The following results should be displayed:

'4'

'8'

'11'

'6'

To use the formula for rounding numbers to one decimal place, only the first condition of the If Statement needs to be amended to 'push' the '5' down one decimal place:

```
numberVar intNumber := 5.45;

If (Truncate(intNumber,1) + 0.05) <> intNumber Then
        Round(intNumber)
Else If Remainder(Truncate(intNumber,0),2) > 0 Then
        RoundUp(intNumber)
Else
        Truncate(intNumber,0);
```

Type Conversion

Why Type Conversion is useful

Fields are represented in Crystal Reports as the same data type as they are held on the database.

When displaying these fields in a report their original data types should usually be suitable. However, when manipulating fields to evaluate or change their contents, there is often a need to change the way the field is represented.

Many of the exercises presented in this book use type conversion as part of their solution, and nearly all the formula in the third Section include type conversion.

On a day to day basis, data is often imported into databases and other storage mediums which are not conducive to reporting, or the same field may be held as a different type on a different table and must be converted in order to create a link between.

NB: These exercises use variables, for a full description of variables and their uses see the Chapter **Using Variables**.

Report Name: Conversion_Examples.rpt

Report Requirement: Demonstrate how to convert fields into different data types.

Report Details:

Table(s)	Fields
Orders	Employee ID
	Customer ID
	Order Amount
	Required Date
Customer_Addresses	Address1

Converting Numbers to Strings

Converting a number into a string is a very common requirement for various reasons, as will become apparent during the rest of this book.

1. Create a formula called "frmTextEmployeeID".

2. Enter the following to change the Employee ID to a string:

    ToText({Orders.Customer ID});

3. Save and close the formula, and place it in the Details Section to the right of the database fields.

4. Preview the report.

The default output for the ToText Function is to display the number with two decimal places and commas every three digits (because of the low values in the Customer ID field they are not visible in this example).

This is not always relevant, and certainly is not in this case.

5. Open the formula called "frmTextEmployeeID", and amend the code to include the following:

    ToText({Orders.Customer ID},0,"");

6. Save and close the formula, preview the report.

NB: Text is automatically formatted to be left justified.

The additional code does two things:

- The ' 0 ' specifies the number of decimal places.

- The ' "" ' are the double quotes that identify the character used to separate larger numbers (in this case, nothing).

NB: The CSTR does the exact same thing as ToText, but is seldom used.

Converting Strings to Numbers

Unfortunately, there are no suitable fields in the Xtreme Database to test the ToNumber Function against.

We can, however, base it on the TextEmployeeID formula created above.

7. Create a formula called "frmNumberEmployeeID".

8. Enter the following to change the Employee ID to a string:

```
ToNumber({@TextEmployeeID});
```

9. Save and close the formula, then place it in the Details Section to the right of the database fields.

10. Preview the report.

NB: Numeric fields are automatically formatted to be right justified.

Unless there is no possibility at all of the field being none numeric, it is prudent to first check the value being converted to ensure that it is actually a number and will not cause an error then the report is run.

11. Open the formula NumberEmployeeID.

12. Amend the code by preceding it with the following check:

```
If IsNumeric({Orders.Customer ID}) = True Then
        ToNumber({@TextEmployeeID});
```

13. Save and close the formula, preview the report.

NB: There is no need for an Else part of the If Statement unless a default value is required for display.

Converting Strings to Dates

Again, there are no suitable fields in the Xtreme Database to test the Date Function against.

For illustration purposes, in lieu of a field, a variable is going to be used.

14. Create a formula called "frmCreateDate".

15. Enter the following to change the string to a date:

```
stringVar strDateString := "29/08/2009";

Date(strDateString);
```

16. Save and close the formula, and place it in the Report Header (as it is a single value there is little value in repeating it).

17. Preview the report.

In a similar way to converting numbers, it is a good idea to check the value being changed to a date to ensure it is a suitable format.

18. Open the formula frmCreateDate.

19. Amend the code by preceding it with the following check:

```
stringVar DateString := "29/08/2009";

If IsDate(DateString) Then
      Date(DateString);
```

20. Save and close the formula, preview the report.

A date is displayed that can take advantage of all the date formatting options available.

NB: In 'real life' if you are assigning a value to a date field there is no need to enter the date as a string and convert it.

NB: To enter the value as a literal date in a formula:

#29/08/2009#

Converting Strings to DateTime

Handling DateTime conversions is almost identical to date conversions. In the case of the above exercise, the same code would be used, but with the following tweaks:

21. Create a formula called "frmCreateDateTime".

22. Enter the following to change the string to a date time field:

```
stringVar DateTimeString := "29/08/2009 23:59:59";

If IsDateTime(DateTimeString) Then
        DateTime(DateTimeString);
```

23. Preview the report.

The formula displays a date field which can be formatted like any database date time field.

Converting Strings to Arrays

Arrays are covered in depth in the Chapter **Arrays** but the conversion method is included here for completeness.

24. Create a formula called "frmstrAddressarray".

25. Enter the following to change the first line of the Address into an array of words separated by the spaces:

```
stringVar array strAddressarray :=
Split({Employee_Addresses.Address1}," ");

strAddressarray[1];
```

26. Save and close the formula, and place it in the Details Section to the right of the database fields.

27. Preview the report.

The first line of the formula uses the Split Function to separate the Address1 field based on spaces in the string.

The separate elements are then placed into the array strAddressarray.

The last line identifies the first element in the array for display.

NB: This function is more useful than it first appears. Especially if there is a requirement to strip out a particular part of a String.

For example, identifying the third part of a period delimited IP address would be tedious using Mid and InStr, but with the Split Function it is a lot easier:

```
Split({PretendTable.PretendIPAddress}, ".")[3];
```

Date and Time Functions

Virtually every report is based on a date range or value of some kind, and in many cases the evaluation of dates or times make up an important factor of the data being displayed.

Fortunately, Crystal Reports provides a wide variety of functions which enable most date manipulations to be done easily, and with a little work even the more complicated requirements can be realised.

Splitting Date Fields

A date field can be broken down into separate units of time, and separate numbers can be built into a date field.

This is useful for completing partial date fields on a database and is also important when it comes to making the most of the built in functions for date ranges in Crystal Reports (See Chapter **Using Date Ranges**).

Report Name: Date_Functions.rpt

Report Requirement: Separate a date field into component parts.

Report Details:

Table(s)	Fields
Orders	Customer ID Order Date Required Date Shipped Date

To illustrate this, the following exercise splits the Required Date field into separate numeric values, then puts them together with different time values.

1. Create a formula called "frmRequiredYear".

2. Enter the following to identify the year:

    Year({Orders.Required Date});

3. Save and close the formula, and place it in the Details Section to the right of the database fields.

4. Create a formula called "frmRequiredMonth".

5. Enter the following to identify the month:

    Month({Orders.Required Date});

6. Save and close the formula, and place it in the Details Section to the right of the database fields.

7. Create a formula called "frmRequiredDay".

8. Enter the following to identify the Day:

    Day({Orders.Required Date});

9. Save and close the formula, and place it in the Details Section to the right of the database fields.

NB: In this exercise the hours and minutes are to be replaced by random numbers. However, these can be extracted in the same manner if required:

    Hour({Orders.Required Date});

    Minute({Orders.Required Date});

10. Create a formula called "frmRequiredDate".

11. Enter the following code to build a date from the separate formulas:

> Date({@RequiredYear},{@RequiredMonth},{@RequiredDay});

12. Save and close the formula, and place it in the Details Section to the right of the database fields

This formula will display the same date as the Required Date field as you would expect. However, each of these formulas can be replaced with any other number that falls within the accepted range of values:

13. Open the frmRequiredDate formula for editing and change the code to the following:

> Date(1978-1,{@RequiredMonth},{@RequiredDay});

14. Save and close the formula.

The date is displayed with a year of 1977 as expected.

NB: This is very handy for reporting on yearly trends.

15. Create a new formula called "frmRandomTime".

16. Enter the following code:

> DateTime({@RequiredYear},{@RequiredMonth},
> {@RequiredDay}, Truncate(rnd() * 24),
> Truncate(rnd() * 60), Truncate(rnd() * 60));

17. Save and close the formula, and place it in the Details Section to the right of the database fields

This formula contains both the date and the time, although the time has to be randomly generated as it is not stored on the database.

NB: Because of the strict formatting rules regarding date and date/time fields, any formula which build dates are very prone to error.

In order to safe guard against any unforeseen anomalies it is prudent to first test whether or not the values supplied fall within the accepted format for a date field.

18. Open the frmRequiredDate formula for editing and change the code to the following:

```
numberVar intMonth := Truncate(rnd() * 15);

Date({@RequiredYear}, intMonth, {@RequiredDay});
```

19. Save and close the formula.

20. Refresh the report.

Unless you are particularly lucky, an error will occur when you refresh the report even though it saved without any problem.

The variable intMonth will occasionally be equal to more than 12. The resulting error stops the entire report from running.

To trap this potential error Crystal Reports has a function called IsDate, which evaluates a string to identify if it matches the values needed for a date field.

21. Open the frmRequiredDate formula for editing and change the code to the following:

```
numberVar intMonth := truncate(rnd() * 15);

If IsDate(ToText({@RequiredYear},0,"") & "," &
ToText(intMonth,0, "") & "," &
ToText({@RequiredDay},0,"")) Then
        Date({@RequiredYear}, intMonth, {@RequiredDay})
Else
```

         Date(0,0,0);

22. Save and close the formula.

23. Refresh the report.

The formula will now display a blank space if it is not a date.

Because the month part of the formula is generated randomly, refresh the report a few times to see different results each time.

NB: IsDate is used purely for date fields. If the date has a time attached to it, use the IsDateTime function in the same manner, but with additional information for the time:

        IsDateTime(ToText ({@RequiredYear},0,"") & "," &
        ToText(intMonth,0, "") & "," & ToText({@RequiredDay},0,"") & "
        21" &":" & "23" & ":" & "13")

Displaying the Month Name

There is often a requirement to display the month by name rather than by number. This is regularly a requirement in report titles. This also helps avoid possible confusion between American and English date formats.

If the title is a textbox with the date field dragged into it, traditional formatting can be used to display the month by its name.

However, if the title is being built via a formula as is often the case (especially when displaying user selections from parameter fields) this formatting needs to be implemented via a formula.

To illustrate both this formatting and how splitting a date field can be used individually: the following exercise prompts the user for a month, then filters the report content based on their choice and displays it in the report title.

1. Create a string parameter called "prmSelectAMonth", with a list of months for default values.

2. Open the Record Selection Formula Editor via the Report Menu and enter the following code to filter the report:

        {?prmSelectAMonth} = MonthName({@RequiredMonth});

3. Save and close the formula.

4. Refresh the report.

The report is limited to those records which have a Required Date within a selected month.

In this particular case, building a title containing the month selected by the user is easily achieved by referencing the prmSelectAMonth parameter.

But to display the month abbreviated to three letters would require more work and the MonthName Function again.

5. Create a formula called "frmReportTitle".

6. Enter the following text with the MonthName Function concatenated to the end:

        "Orders Report for The Month Of " &
        MonthName({@RequiredMonth},True)

7. Save and close the formula.

8. Place the frmReportTitle formula in the Report Header.

9. Preview the report. It may be necessary to resize the formula to view the contents.

The formula will display the month abbreviated to three characters because of the "True" in the MonthName Function.

A date field can be formatted to show the month's name using the formatting options.

Days by Name

In a manner similar to that used to display the month name, the day of the week can also be shown by name.

This is particularly useful in the case of days as many reports measure the number of working days elapsed.

Of course, unlike with months where the January is always identified as 01, the number identifying a day often changes week by week.

Unfortunately, while there is a WeekDayName Function, it operates based on a number one to seven and not the date. There is, however a DayOfWeek Function which allocates a number to each day based on its position within the week.

NB: The DayOfWeek starts with Sunday as the first day of the week. This can be changed within the formula.

Using the frmRandomDate formula from the previous exercise, we are going to create a formula to identify the day for the frmRequiredYear formula.

1. Create a new formula called frmRequiredDayName.

2. Enter the following code to identify the correct day:

```
If DayOfWeek({@RandomDate}) > 0 Then
        WeekDayName(DayOfWeek({@RandomDate}))
Else
        "Invalid Date";
```

3. Save and close the formula and insert it into the Detail Section.

4. Refresh the report.

As the formula is based on a random date, the results will change on every refresh.

NB: The DayOfWeek Function uses the whole date field to calculate when the actual day falls, unlike MonthName which requires the month to be stripped out of the date field.

Measuring Time Elapsed between Dates

Displaying how much time has elapsed between two dates is the basis of many reports, especially those which measure service performance, or in the case of this exercise, the number of days between an order being placed and when the order was shipped.

There are two different ways to do this:

* Subtract one date from the other in the same way as with numbers.

  This works because Crystal Reports will use days as the default for calculating the result. It is far from ideal and will not work for months or any other time measurement.

  I am including it only because it is a common 'cheat' and it is likely that it will be encountered when amending other people's reports.

* Using the DateDiff function which enables various units of time between two dates to be measured, from seconds to years.

For illustration purposes, the first formula is based on the first method.

Report Name: Date_Comparisons.rpt

Report Requirement: Show the uses of date and time ranges and comparisons.

Report Details:

Table(s)	Fields
Orders	Customer ID Order Date Required Date Shipped Date

1. Create a formula called "frmQuickDays".

2. Enter the following code:

    {Orders.Ship Date}-{Orders.Order Date};

3. Save and close the formula.

4. Insert the formula frmQuickDays into the Details Section and refresh the report.

The number of days elapsed between the two dates is displayed.

By default, any partial units are displayed as decimal values. So 36 hours measured in days would be: 1.50, not 1.12 as may be expected.

See **Elapsed Time in Minutes and Seconds** for an explanation of how to display the results from DateDiff in more than one unit of time.

To get the same result using DateDiff:

5. Create a formula called "frmDiffDays".

6. Enter the following code:

```
DateDiff("d",{Orders.Order Date},{Orders.Ship Date});
```

7. Save and close the formula.

8. Insert the formula frmDiffDays into the Details Section and refresh the report.

NB: DateDiff truncates any fractions of the unit being measured (in this case Days).

The difference between the two methods seems negligable, until there is a need to measure the time difference in another unit.

In this case, an additional formula is going to measure the difference in seconds.

1. Create a formula called "frmDiffSeconds".

2. Enter the following code:

```
DateDiff("s",{Orders.Order Date},{Orders.Ship Date});
```

3. Save and close the formula.

4. Insert the formula "frmDiffSeconds" into the Details Section and refresh the report.

The only difference between this formula and frmDiffDays is that the interval type has been changed from "d" for days, to "s" for seconds.

A full range of unit types are available:

DateDiff Abbreviation	Unit Returned
yyyy	Year
q	Quarter
m	Month
d	Day
w	Weeks
h	Hour
n	Minute
s	Second

NB: 'n' is the abbreviation for minutes.

In addition, see **Counting Working Days Between Two Dates** for how to only count the working days between two dates using both DateDiff and DayOfWeek.

NB: DateDiff is used in many other chapters within this book as it has various applications beyond just displaying elapsed time.

Manipulating Date Values

Another particularly useful function is DateAdd which can be used to both increase and decrease a date by the same units available to DateDiff.

In the following exercise, two days are going to be added to the shipping date.

1.   Create a formula called "frmDateOffSet".

2.   Enter the following code:

```
DateAdd("D",2,{Orders.Ship Date});
```

3. Save and close the formula.

4. Insert the formula frmDateOffSet into the Details Section and refresh the report.

Two days are added to the shipping date.

To add two months, it is just a matter of changing the type of unit which is being increased:

5. Open the formula frmDateOffSet for editing.

6. Amend the code to the following by changing the "D" to an "M":

    DateAdd("M",2,{Orders.Ship Date});

7. Save and close the formula.

NB: When relevant, the function will increase the year also.

There is not a DateMinus or DateSubtract Function. To deduct from a Date (there is not a DateDeduct Function either!) enter a negative value in the DateAdd.

To lower the Shipping Date by two quarters, do the following:

8. Open the formula frmDateOffSet for editing.

9. Amend the code to the following by changing the "M" to an "Q":

    DateAdd("Q",-2,{Orders.Ship Date});

10. Save and close the formula.

A common requirement when dealing with this kind of date manipulation like this is to increase the value by more than one unit of time.

The following exercise gives a quick demonstration on how it works.

The shipping date is going to be increased by one month and three days.

11. Create a formula called "frmNestedDateOffSet" and enter the following code:

```
DateAdd("D",3,{Orders.Ship Date}));
```

12. Enter the following code before the existing function:

```
DateAdd("M",1,
```

13. Enter a closing bracket ')' just before the semi colon to close the second DateAdd Function:

```
DateAdd("M",1,DateAdd("D",3,{Orders.Ship Date}));
```

14. Save and close the formula.

15. Preview the report.

Because the first DateAdd Function returns a date (with three days added) it is accepted as a date by the second DateAdd Function which then adds one month to that result.

Using Date Ranges

An extensive collection of date ranges are available to enable quick comparisons between dates and certain time spans.

A date range is a pre-set array of dates (For more on arrays see the **Arrays** Chapter). These allow a single date to be compared with a range of dates at once.

Report Name: Date_Ranges.rpt

Report Requirement: Use date ranges for a variety of tasks.

Additional Setup: Due to the nature of these tutorials, some work is required to provide useful dates to work with in the following exercise.

Depending on the version of Crystal Reports being used and the sample database that shipped with it, the date values can be years out of date. Also, I don't know when you, the reader, are going to work through this particular tutorial: so I am reluctant to suggest specific dates in the text.

Report Details:

Table(s)	Fields
Orders	Customer ID

The short initial exercise is to create a usable date field which is relevant regardless of when the next tutorial is undertaken.

1. Create a formula called "frmTestDate".

2. Enter the following code to set up random date values:

```
numberVar intDay := Truncate(Rnd () * Day(Today)+1);
numberVar intMonth := Truncate (Rnd () * Month(Today)+1);
numberVar intYear := Truncate (Rnd () * 2);
```

3. Follow this with the code to build the random values into a useable date format:

```
Date(ToText(intDay,0,"") & "/" &  ToText(intMonth,0,"") &
"/" & ToText(Year(Today)-intYear,0,""));
```

4. Save and close the formula.

5. Insert the formula frmTestDate to the extreme left of the Details Section and refresh the report.

Because this formula creates random values based on the Special Field 'Today', it will always produce dates relevant to when you are running the report.

The following exercise is going create a series of different formulas, each of which state whether or not the frmTestDate formula falls within a specific range.

This selection of date ranges will cover most reporting requirements needed in day to day reporting.

1. Create a formula called "frmWithinLastWeek".

2. Enter the following code:

```
If {@frmTestDate} In Last7Days Then
        "Within One Week"
Else
        "Not Within One Week";
```

3. Save and close the formula.

4. Insert the formula into the Details Section.

5. Create a formula called "frmWithinLastFullmonth".

6. Enter the following code:

```
If {@frmTestDate} In LastFullMonth Then
        "Within Last Full Month"
Else
        "Not Within Last Full Month";
```

7. Save and close the formula.

8. Insert the formula frmWithinLastFullmonth into the Details Section.

9. Create a formula called "frmWithinThismonth".

10. Enter the following code:

```
If {@frmTestDate} In MonthToDate Then
        "Within This Month"
Else
        "Not Within This Month";
```

11. Save and close the formula.

12. Insert the formula frmWithinThismonth into the Details Section.

13. Create a formula called "frmWithinThisYear".

14. Enter the following code:

```
If {@frmTestDate} In YearToDate Then
        "Within This Year"
Else
        "Not Within This Year";
```

15. Save and close the formula.

16. Insert the formula frmWithinThisYear into the Details Section.

17. Preview the report.

NB: The time of year at which you are running the report will affect the likelihood of a particular formula showing a positive result.

While there are many more date ranges than those used in this exercise, the examples worked through should give the general idea of their uses.

Many reports need to be based on a rolling basis of the past twelve months. This can be realised via two date ranges (depending on specific requirements):

- LastYearMTD

- LastYearYTD

Manipulation of Additional Date Ranges

The list available of date ranges is extensive, but not inclusive.

A report required to display the dates which fall within the previous two months is not catered for and will need additional work to develop.

As previously stated, date ranges are arrays. This means that they can be treated in a similar manner.

Particularly useful are the Maximum and Minimum Functions, especially when used in conjunction with the DateAdd Function.

The following exercise realises the above example of identifying which dates are within the last two full months.

1. Create a formula called "frmWithin2FullMonths".

2. Enter the following code:

```
If {@frmTestDate} In
DateAdd("M",-1,Minimum(LastFullMonth)) To
Maximum(LastFullMonth) Then
```

3. Complete the code:

```
        "Within Last Two Full Months"
Else
        "Not Within Last Two Full Months";
```

4. Save and close the formula.

5. Insert the formula frmWithin2FullMonths into the Details Section.

After the 'To' is self explanatory and takes the last date of the last full month:

```
Maximum(LastFullMonth)
```

The code before the 'To' is a little more involved:

```
DateAdd("M",-1,Minimum(LastFullMonth))
```

First, the Minimum Function takes the earliest date in the last full month.

The DateAdd then deducts a month from this date.

Using date ranges in this manner, greatly increases their scope and usefulness.

Additionally, different date ranges can be used in the same comparison of a date.

In the previous exercise, LastFullMonth was used, but if the requirement was to identify dates within all of the last full month and the current month two main solutions are commonly used.

In both cases, the code before the 'To' should be:

Minimum(LastFullMonth)

After the 'To', a similar means of determining the current Date is:

Minimum(LastFullMonth) To Maximum(MonthToDate)

However, a simple (and often used) solution is to use the Special Field Today:

Minimum(LastFullMonth) To Today

A Warning about Date Formats

The format in which a date field is actually displayed should always be explicitly specified via the Format Editor or via the Fields Tab on the Options window.

Do not rely on the 'System Default Long format' or 'System Default Short format' as these can change from system to system.

Another thing to watch is the order in which Crystal Reports is handling the day and month.

Again this can be set field by field, or using the Options window, but when creating literal values it is best to either use the Date Function or entering the month as text:

#01/03/2009#

The above could be the first of March, or the third of January.

This confusion is further compounded as the following date:

#01/24/2009#

Would be accepted as the 24th of January without error, as would this date:

#24/01/2009#

And even if the following code was written:

Today In [#24/01/2009# To #01/03/2009#];

There is no guarantee that both dates would be treated the same. But there is no question which it is with the following:

#01/MARCH/2009#

Always err on the side of caution when using dates.

Using Variables

Variables and Their Uses

If you are working through this book in order, you will have already used variables to complete some of the exercises. While it is possible to create a lot of formulas without them, it is not long before they are required.

A variable is a piece of memory which temporarily stores a value while the report is running.

In all practical terms, a variable is a database field created within the report and everything which was true in Chapter **Database Fields** for database fields of a particular data type is also true for a variable of the same type.

There is a variable type for each of the major database field types with a few exceptions and generalisations:

- Memo Fields

  Some of the older versions of Crystal Reports do not handle memo fields within formula (though they can be included directly in reports).

  If the formula can't use memo fields, any fields of that type will not be visible within the listed fields within the formula.

- Single / Integer / Long Fields

  All of the above are grouped together and treated as the number data type. This happens in the report as a whole, and not just in the Formula Editor.

When and How to use a Variable

Variables are used throughout the exercises in this book whenever they are required to meet a practical need.

As a general rule, it is appropriate to use a variable at any time you want to store a value within a formula for later use, either within that formula, or elsewhere.

The following tutorials however, use variables in an abstract way designed to demonstrate their abilities, rather than in the practical context.

Variable Syntax

A variable must be set up before it can be used, and while this can be done at any point in a formula it is good practice to always create them at the top before any other code.

By selecting the required variable from the Variable Declarations folder and double clicking it, a 'template' will appear in the Code Panel in the same way as double clicking a function will:

    dateVar := ;

To create an empty variable to be populated by the formula code to follow, delete the ':=' and enter a name for the variable:

    dateVar DateVariable;

Alternatively, to create a variable that has a value the instant it is created, use the ':=' to assign it:

    dateVar DateVariable := #22/05/2009#;

NB: It is not possible to create your own constants in Crystal Reports formulas.

Report Name: Variable_uses.rpt

Report Requirement: The various uses of variables.

Report Details:

Table(s)	Fields
Orders	Order Amount Employee ID Required Date Payment Received Courier Website Ship Via

String Variables

String variables are the equivalent of string database fields and can be used to store literal text, or the contents of a field or fields.

The following exercise demonstrates many of the ways a string variable can be used.

1. Create a formula called "frmStringVariables".

2. Enter the following code to set up the string variable:

```
stringVar strTestVariable;
```

3. Save and close the formula.

4. Place the formula in the Detail Section and preview the report.

The formula is empty as it is equal to the variable strTestVariable, which is empty.

5. Reopen the formula and add amend the code to:

```
stringVar strTestVariable := "Literal Value";
```

5. Save and close the formula and preview the report.

The formula now displays the text: "Literal Value", as that is the variable's contents.

6. Reopen the formula and add the following code to the end:

```
strTestVariable := "Different Literal Value";
```

7. Save and close the formula and preview the report.

The formula now displays the text: "Different Literal Value", because that value has been used to replace the variable's original contents.

8. Reopen the formula and add the following code to the end:

```
strTestVariable := strTestVariable & " and the Field
Courier Website: ";
```

9. Save and close the formula and preview the report.

The formula now displays the text:

```
"Different Literal Value and the Field Courier Website: "
```

Because additional text has been joined (concatenated) to the original value and then assigned to the variable.

10. Reopen the formula and add the following code to the end:

```
strTestVariable := strTestVariable & {Orders.Courier
Website};
```

11. Save and close the formula and preview the report.

Once more, the formula runs through each line of the formula in turn and displays the text:

"Different Literal Value and the Field Courier Website: "

Together with the Website field because fields that are strings can be concatenated in the same manner as other text.

12. Reopen the formula and add the following code to the end:

"Not The Variable";

13. Save and close the formula and preview the report.

The text: "Not The Variable", is displayed. The variable's contents have not changed from the previous step, but are not shown as they are not the last thing in the formula.

14. Reopen the formula and add the following code to the end:

strTestVariable := UpperCase(strTestVariable);

15. Save and close the formula and preview the report.

The variable contents from step 10 are all switched into upper case and displayed.

16. Reopen the formula and add the following code to the end:

ProperCase(strTestVariable);

17. Save and close the formula and preview the report.

The first letter in each word is now upper case. This is displayed in the formula as it is the last thing to be done, even though it is not assigned to the variable.

18. Reopen the formula and add the following code to the end:

> strTestVariable := ToText({Orders.Employee ID},0,"");

19. Save and close the formula and preview the report.

The variable contents are replaced with the Employee ID, which is a number and so needs converting to be assigned to the string variable.

20. Reopen the formula and add the following code to the end:

> strTestVariable := "Employee ID: " & {Orders.Employee ID};

21. Save and close the formula and preview the report.

When a number is concatenated to text before being assigned to a string variable it is converted automatically. However, the number will be displayed with the default settings of two decimal places and comma separated numbers.

Number Variables

1. Create a formula called "frmNumberTests".

2. Enter the following code to set up the number variable:

> numberVar intTestVariable;

3. Save and close the formula.

4. Place the formula in the Detail Section and preview the report.

The formula will display: "0.00", as the variable is empty and that is the default value.

NB: Number formulas are right hand justified by default.

5. Reopen the formula and amend the existing code to:

numberVar intTestVariable := 72;

6. Save and close the formula and preview the report.

The number: "72.00" is displayed as this now the value assigned to the variable.

7. Reopen the formula and add the following code to the end:

intTestVariable := 3;

8. Save and close the formula and preview the report.

"3.00" is now displayed due to the number '3' being assigned to the variable after the '72'.

9. Reopen the formula and add the following code to the end:

intTestVariable := 2 * 9.55;

10. Save and close the formula and preview the report.

The formula evaluates the calculation of 2 multiplied by 9.55, then assigned the result to the variable, so the formula displays "19.10".

11. Reopen the formula and add the following code to the end:

intTestVariable := (2 + 9) * 3;

12. Save and close the formula and preview the report.

Normal mathematic rules apply and 2 will be added to 9 and the result multiplied by 3 and then assigned to the variable as the final value of "33".

13. Reopen the formula and add the following code to the end:

```
intTestVariable := 7/4;
```

14. Save and close the formula and preview the report.

"1.75" is displayed, superseding all previous values and making use of the two decimal places.

15. Reopen the formula and add the following code to the end:

```
intTestVariable := intTestVariable * 8;
```

16. Save and close the formula and preview the report.

The variable's current content of "1.75" is multiplied by 8 and the result of "14" is assigned to the variable and displayed as "14.00".

17. Reopen the formula and add the following code to the end:

```
67;
```

18. Save and close the formula and preview the report.

In the same way as the string variable, the number variable is ignored as the number "67" is the last thing to be evaluated by the formula, and so "67.00" is displayed.

19. Reopen the formula and add the following code to the end:

```
intTestVariable := SQR(intTestVariable);
```

20. Save and close the formula and preview the report.

The variable value is still set at 14 from step 15, even though the variable is set to 67.

The SQR Function is used to find the square root of this value, which is then assigned to the variable over the original value.

The number "3.74" is displayed.

21. Reopen the formula and add the following code to the end:

```
Truncate(intTestVariable);
```

22. Save and close the formula and preview the report.

The Truncate Function removes everything after the decimal point.

However, the number is still displayed with two decimal places due to formatting, so "3.00" is displayed.

It should now be apparent that there are a lot of similarities in how variables behave regardless of their type.

The following exercises focus more on the specific differences between the variable types.

Date, Time and DateTime Variables

Three time based variables exist, all of which are similar enough to be treated as one subject:

- Date

- Time

- DateTime

The following exercise highlights the common rules and differences between these variable types:

1. Create a formula called "frmDateTests".

2. Enter the following code:

```
datetimeVar dteTestVariable;

dteTestVariable := #23/01/2010#;
```

3. Save and close the formula.

4. Place the formula in the Detail Section and preview the report.

The actual value displayed is "23/01/2010 00:00:00" (though this may vary depending on system settings). This is because Crystal Reports populates the empty time part of the variable with a default value.

This is also true when loading a database field that is a date into a DateTime variable.

NB: This is a common cause of a lot of errors when using dates within filters.

5. Enter the following code:

```
dteTestVariable := #23/01/2010 12:00:00#;
```

6. Save and close the formula.

The actual value displayed is "23/01/2010 12:00:00" (again, this may vary depending on system settings).

7. Open the formula and insert the additional two lines so the code looks like this:

```
datetimeVar dteTesttimeVariable;
dateVar dteTestVariable;

dteTesttimeVariable := #23/01/2010#;
```

---

        dteTesttimeVariable := #23/01/2010 12:00:00#;

        dteTestVariable := #23/01/2010 12:00:00#;

   8. Click on the 'Check' icon.

The code errors, complaining that #23/01/2010# is not a date. This seems a really strange error, especially as the same value was accepted earlier in step 2.

However, the # symbol denotes a date and time value and when used to populate a DateTime Crystal Report adds a default time value if none exists.

For a date time variable to accept #23/01/2010# it must be converted into a date type.

NB: A value of #23/01/2010 12:00:00# would also error when passed to a date variable and would need the same conversion as shown below:

   9. Amend the last line of code to:

        dteVariable := Date(#23/01/2010 12:00:00#);

   10. Save and close the formula.

The date value is displayed successfully without a time element.

   11. Insert the following code, the first line at the top of the formula, the second line at the end:

        timeVar TimeTestVariable;

        TimeTestVariable := TIME(#10:10:00#);

   12. Save and close the formula.

In a similar manner to the how a date value is passed to date variable, the same method is used to pass a time into a time variable.

Boolean (True/False) Variables

A boolean variable can hold three values; True, False and Null.

However, Null cannot be directly assigned as a value, but can be passed into the report from the database.

1. Create a variable called "frmBlnTests".

2. Enter the following code:

```
booleanVar blnTestVariable;
```

3. Save and close the formula, insert it into the Detail Section and preview the report.

The formula will display the default value for a boolean variable with is 'False'.

4. Reopen the formula and add the following code to the end:

```
blnTestVariable := True;
```

5. Save and close the formula and preview the report.

As expected, 'True' is displayed in the report.

6. Reopen the formula and add the following code to the end:

```
blnTestVariable := 2 = 2;
```

7. Save and close the formula and preview the report.

The variable will hold the result of anything after the ':=' in the same way as a number variable will hold the results of a division or a string variable holds concatenated text.

So in this case, because 2 is equal to 2, the value 'True' will be displayed.

8. Reopen the formula and add the following code to the end:

        blnTestVariable := 2 = 3;

9. Save and close the formula and preview the report.

In this case, because 2 is not equal to 3, the value 'False' will be displayed.

10. Reopen the formula and add the following code to the end:

        blnTestVariable := {Orders.Ship Date} >=
        {Orders.Required Date};

11. Save and close the formula and preview the report.

The formula will display 'True' if an order has shipped on, or after the required date. Alternatively, it will display 'False' if shipped before the required date.

Changing the title for this formula to "Orders Shipped Late" provides a meaningful context to the formula and the use of Boolean variables.

Boolean tests are particularly useful for conditional formatting. This is covered in the Chapter **Conditional Formatting with Formulas**.

Currency Variables

The difference between currency variables and number variables are negligable.

A currency variable is declared like this:

    currencyVar curTestVariable;

For examples of the correct use of this variable, refer to the Number Variable exercises previously covered.

NB: Some functions which work with number variables, will not work with currency variables. If this occurs, use the ToNumber Function to change the data type and CCUR to change it back after any calculations.

Array Variables

An array variable can hold several values at once and is not a variable data type in its own right but rather a collection of the standard types already discussed. So a string array is a collection of strings, a number array is a collection of numbers and so on.

Array variables are declared in the same manner as other variables, but with the addition of the word 'array' after the date type:

    numberVar array arrayNumber := [1,2,3,4,5,6];

Or:

    stringVar array arrayString := ["a","b","a","grt","g"];

It is almost impossible not to use variables when dealing with arrays, and this is covered in great detail in the **Array** Chapter.

Range Variables

Range variables are a variation of the array variable, but rather than listing each item only the first value and the last is provided.

        numberVar range rngNumber := 1 to 6;

Or:

        stringVar range rngString := "a" to "f";

Ranges are also covered in the **Ranges** Chapter.

Variable Scope and Types

Scope refers to where the variable can be 'seen' or accessed within the report and possibly subreports. Scope is a lot more important than is apparent at first.

Three different types of scope exist:

- Local
- Global
- Shared

Local

A variable can only be used within the formula where it is declared.

The keyword 'Local' is typed before any variable declaration to restrict the scope:

        Local numberVar intTestVariable;

Global

The default scope is Global, if none is explicitly entered.

So far, all variable declarations in the previous exercises have been Global because no scope has been specified:

        numberVar intTestVariable;

This is the same as:

        Global numberVar intTestVariable;

Because the default scope for a variable is Global, which means that any variable without a specified scope will be visible to other formula and will be affected accordingly.

This, and the potential resulting problems, are illustrated in detail in Chapter **Correct Formula Order**.

Shared

Strangely, the Shared scope is more 'global' than the Global scope. A Shared variable can be passed between formulas within a report, and can also be passed to formula in subreports.

Shared variables are declared like so:

        Shared numberVar intTestVariable;

The next chapter shows how this scope is used in reporting.

Passing Variables between Formulas

Using Global and Shared Variables

Being able to transfer a value from one formula to another can often be the only way to solve some requirements. There are many examples of this within the more complex formula solutions in Section Three of this book.

However, in this exercise, the emphasis is on how Global variables work in their own right, rather than as part of a complex solution.

Report Name: Variables_Between_Formulas.rpt

Report Requirement: Show the how different scope types alter formula results. The database table is used only to generate multiple Detail rows.

Report Details:

Table(s)	Fields
Orders	Customer ID

1. Create a formula called "frmSetupVariable".

2. Enter the following code:

```
Global numberVar intVariable := 5;
```

3. Save and close the formula, insert it into the Report Header Section and preview the report.

The formula will display the number 5 as expected.

4. Create a formula called "frmShowVariable".

5. Enter the following code:

```
Global numberVar intVariable;
```

6. Save and close the formula, insert it into the Report Footer Section and preview the report.

This formula will also display the number 5 because the variable intVariable was assigned the value 5 in the previous formula.

7. Reopen the formula frmShowVariable and add the following code to the end:

```
intVariable := intVariable + 5;
```

8. Save and close the formula and preview the report.

The formula frmShowVariable now displays 10, the original value of the variable set in frmSetupVariable, and the 5 added to it in frmShowVariable.

NB: frmSetupVariable still displays the value 5 and has not been updated as the formula frmShowVariable is evaluated after frmSetupVariable due to being in a different location physically in the report.

9. Reopen the formula frmSetupVariable and add the following code to the end:

```
IntVariable := 10;
```

10. Save and close the formula and preview the report.

Both formulas are displayed with their values increased by 5.

11. Insert another copy of the frmShowVariable formula into the Detail Section.

12. Preview the report.

The copy of the frmShowVariable formula in the Detail Section, starts with a value of 10, and increments by 5 each row of the report.

Additionally, the frmShowVariable in the Report Footer is equal to the last frmShowVariable formula plus the additional 5 it adds to the total.

NB: This exercise will work in exactly the same way if the variable is declared with a Shared scope instead of Global.

13. Highlight the formula frmSetupVariable on the report page and delete it.

The frmShowVariable value will now be displayed minus the 10 it was assigned in the frmSetupVariable.

NB: A formula which manipulates a variable (including declaring it) must be physically within the actual report for it to have an effect. A formula can be suppressed to hide it from view when a report is previewed.

Specifying When Formulas are Calculated

Occasionally, when formulas refer to each other, the order in which Crystal Reports evaluates becomes very important.

When using variables to pass information between formulas the likelihood of a problem occurring increases.

As a general rule, it is good practice to use the EvaluateAfter Function in any formula that is dependent on another formula.

The EvaluateAfter Function is simple enough to use and should be the first line of the formula:

EvaluateAfter(???);

….where the question marks are replaced with the name of the formula which needs to be evaluated first.

NB: EvaluateAfter is located in the 'Evaluation Time' directory in the Function Panel. But if added to the formula code by double clicking or drag and drop, it does not have the required semi colon, so one must be added manually.

Best Practice for Declaring Scopes

Ideally, the scope for each variable should be implicitly stated in every formula. As we've seen, even in simple reports, the default Global scope makes it easy for variable names to cause erroneous results.

As a general rule, any variable which is only ever going to be used within one formula should be declared Local in scope. This is especially important if reports are likely to be modified by more than one person.

Control Structures

Control structures provide the formulas with the ability to make decisions on what and how to manipulate data.

It is so difficult to write useful formula without control structures. Some of the more simple ones have already been used in previous exercises.

Using If Statements

The If Statement is the simplest way to control how a formula will behave, but can be built into complex solutions if required.

An If Statement works by comparing two or more values, and if they match, performing a particular action. It the values don't match, either no action is performed, or an alternative action takes place.

Report Name: Control_Structures.rpt

Report Requirement: The object of this report is to demonstrate all the variations of If Statements from the most simple, to the highly complex.

Report Details:

Table(s)	Fields
Employee	Employee ID Position Last Name First Name

1. Create a formula called "frmIfStatement".

2. Enter the following code:

```
If {Employees.EmployeeID} > 4 Then
        "Option 1: Employee ID 5 or more.";
```

3. Save and close the formula.

4. Insert the formula in the Detail Section and preview the report.

The formula is empty until the Employee ID is greater than four, at which point the Text "Option 1: Employee ID 5 or more." is displayed.

To display text for Employee ID's are under five, an additional condition needs adding to the If Statement in the form of an Else.

5. Open the formula frmIfStatement and amend the code to match the following:

```
If {Employees.EmployeeID} > 4 Then
        "Option 1: Employee ID 5 or more."
Else
        "Option 2: Employee ID less than 5.";
```

6. Save and close the formula, preview the report.

Now, if the condition is false, the If Statement will display: "Option 2: Employee ID less than 5.".

When more than two options are required; the If Statement can be extended to include addition conditions.

7. Open the formula frmIfStatement and amend the code to match the following:

```
If {Employees.EmployeeID} > 4 Then
        "Option 1: Employee ID 5 or more."
Else If {Employees.EmployeeID} > 2 Then
        "Option 2: Employee ID between 2 and 5."
Else
        "Option 3: Employee ID less than 3.";
```

8. Save and close the formula, preview the report.

The If Statement now has a second comparison which displays "Option 2: Employee ID between 2 and 5."

The final Else displays "Option 3: Employee ID less than 3." for customer ID's of 1 or 2.

NB: It is possible to have an endless list of Else If's. However, it is considered poor practice if this is done to evaluate the same field each time,and if this is the case a Select Case should be used instead.

Each If / Else If does not have to be based on the same field, and in some cases, using mixed fields can simpllfy a complex evaluation.

The logic to identify Employees with an Employee ID greater than four who are Sales Representatives can be evaluated with a minimum of code.

9. Create a new formula called "frmIfStatementExtended" and add the following code:

```
If {Employees.EmployeeID} < 5 Then
        "Option 1: Employee ID less than 5."
Else If {Employees.Title} = "Sales Representative" Then
        "Option 2: Both Conditions Met"
Else
        "Option 3: Right Employee ID, wrong Job Title.";
```

10. Save and close the formula, preview the report.

Because the first comparison looks for the opposite of the condition required (i.e.: an Employee ID greater than four), the second part will only be evaluated if the first part is false.

It is often the case that more than one line of code needs to be evaluated as the result of an If Statement.

To do this, the numerous lines must be within brackets.

The formula needs updating to add 1000 to the Employee ID and then concatenate that number to the employee last name when both conditions are true.

11. Open the formula frmIfStatementExtended and amend the code to match the following:

```
numberVar EmployeeID := 1000;

If {Employees.EmployeeID} < 5 Then
        "Option 1: Employee ID less than 5."
Else If {Employees.Title} = "Sales Representative" Then
(
        EmployeeID := EmployeeID +
        {Employees.EmployeeID};

        {Employees.LastName} & " " &
        ToText(EmployeeID,0,"");
)
Else
        "Option 3: Right Employee ID, wrong Job Title.";
```

12. Save and close the formula, preview the report.

Brackets have only been used in the first part of the If Statement which holds multiple (two in this case) lines of code, but single lines can be bracketed without problems.

NB: This exercise is to demonstrate using brackets, but could have been realised without the variable and using only one line of code instead of two within the If Statement:

```
{Employees.LastName}
& " " &
ToText(1000+{Employees.EmployeeID},0,"")
```

As may be apparent, If Statements can get quite complicated, quite quickly. But the underlying logic is always the same and can be followed through with some time and effort.

Balancing If Statements

Because a formula is treated like a database field by Crystal Reports, it can only be one data type. As a result, an If Statement can only evaluate to one data type.

To illustrate this, to create an If Statement which displays the Employee ID if it is five or more, or otherwise,to display the job title, should be straight forward enough.

1. Create a new formula called "frmIfBalancing".

2. Enter the following code:

```
If {Employees.EmployeeID} > 4 Then
        {Employees.EmployeeID}
Else
        {Employees.Title};
```

3. Check the formula.

The formula will display the message:

"A number is required here."

As a rule, Crystal Reports will always highlight the second part of an If Statement as being wrong. In this case however, while it is easy to change the Employee ID to text to balance the If Statement, changing the highlighted Title Field to a number is impossible.

4. Amend the code to the following:

```
If {Employees.EmployeeID} > 4 Then
        ToText({Employees.EmployeeID},0,"")
Else
        {Employees.Title};
```

5. Save and close the formula.

6. Insert the formula in the Detail Section and preview the report.

The formula will now save without error and behave as expected.

Multiple lines of code bracketed within an If Statement can cause unexpected balancing issues, especially when being used to populate a variable for later use within the formula.

1. Create a new formula called "frmIfCheat".

2. Enter the following code:

```
numberVar numEmployeeID := {Employees.EmployeeID};
stringVar strEmployeeName := {Employees.LastName};

If {Employees.EmployeeID} > 4 Then
(
        numEmployeeID := numEmployeeID + 1000;
)
Else
(
        strEmployeeName := {Employees.LastName} & ", "
        & {Employees.FirstName};
);

strEmployeeName & " " & ToText(numEmployeeID,0,"");
```

3. Save and close the formula.

Once more, the formula displays the same error as before. The problem is basically the same - the If Statement does not balance.

However, in this case, the If Statement is assigning values to variables and the last line of code (the one that is always displayed) is always the same.

Because of this, either side of the Else can be altered to make the If Statement balance.

4. Open the formula called frmIfCheat and amend the If Statement to the following (leaving the variable declaration, and the last line of the formula unchanged):

```
If {Employees.EmployeeID} > 4 Then
(
        numEmployeeID := numEmployeeID + 1000;
        "Bit Of Text To Fool Crystal Reports";
)
Else
(
        strEmployeeName := {Employees.LastName} & ", "
        & {Employees.FirstName};
);
```

5. Save and close the formula.

6. Insert the formula in the Detail Section and preview the report.

The additional text, while doing nothing functionally, means both sides of the Else are both text.

Of course it is equally valid to change the text side of the Else to a number.

7. Open the formula called frmIfCheat and amend the If Statement to the following (leaving the variable declaration and the last line of the formula unchanged):

```
If {Employees.EmployeeID} > 4 Then
(
        EmployeeID := EmployeeID + 1000;
)
Else
(
```

```
            EmployeeName := {Employees.LastName} & ", " &
            {Employees.FirstName};
            1;
      );
```

8. Save and close the formula.

The addition of the number one, also does nothing functionally, but balances both sides of the Else as numbers.

Not Using If Statements for Simple Comparisons

While If Statements are considered best practice for evaluating conditions and provide complete control, in cases where very simple comparisons are needed it is possible to evaluate without using the If Statement structure.

When a formula only needs to return True or False, such as in a selection formula, Running Total or Suppress formula, a simple comparison of values will yield the same result:

```
{Orders.Order Date} = {Orders.Ship Date};
```

This will give identify which Orders were shipped the same day as they were ordered, just the same end result as:

```
If {Orders.Order Date} = {Orders.Ship Date} Then
    True
Else
    False;
```

Problems arise, however, when trying to identify which records are not equal:

```
{Orders.Order Date} <> {Orders.Ship Date};
```

This formula will return False if the dates are equal, and True if they are not. But, if the Shipping Date is Null, the formula will return Null and exclude the record, despite the fields not being equal.

This can cause very misleading reports, but can be handled easy with the If Statement approach:

```
If IsNull({Orders.Ship Date}) Then
        True
Else If {Orders.Order Date} <> {Orders.Ship Date} Then
        True
```

                Else
                        False;

So while simple comparisons can work in some instances, be careful not to overuse them, and when in doubt, use If Statements.

Using Order of Processing

To simpllfy the conditions of an If Statement or Select Case Statement it is possible in many instances it is possible to use the order in which Crystal Reports processes conditional statements.

In the following formula a random number is passed in through the x variable, and then compares it to five number ranges and sets the resulting color:

```
numberVar x := Rnd();

If x In [0.0 to  0.20] then
        Color (238,0,0)
Else If x In [21 to  0.40] then
        Color (235,124,0)
Else If x In [0.41 to 0.60] then
        Color (255,198,0)
Else If x In [0.61 to 0.80] then
        Color (126,159,223)
Else If x > 0.80 then
        Color(190,75,190);
```

But because the formula takes the first condition that matches, if x is 0.10, the formula will not evaluate the rest of the If Statement.

Knowing this, a far quicker to write and easier to maintain formula can be written:

```
numberVar x;

If x < 0.21 Then
   Color(238,0,0)
Else If x <  0.41 Then
   Color(235,124,0)
Else If x < 0.61 Then
   Color(255,198,0)
```

```
        Else If x < 0.81 Then
            Color(126,159,223)
        Else
            Color(190,75,190);
```

Again, assuming x is 0.10, the formula will stop evaluating on the first condition, even though x would test true for all the If conditions.

NB: When working on reports developed by others, it is quite common to see:

```
        If x > 0.0 And x < 0.21 then
            Color(238,0,0)
            ......
```

This is particularly long winded and again, can easily be replaced with an If Statement using the order of evaluation.

Nested If Statements

The standard If Statement allows for a straightforward True or False evaluation which, shown previously, can be realised in a much simpler fashion.

The value of If Statements is that can be nested (ie an If Statement can be placed within an existed If Statement) to provide a variety of logical solutions that greatly extends the usefulness of the If Statement and can provide solutions to the most complex of requirements.

In the same way as functions can contain other functions, If Statements can contain other If Statements.

Report Name: Nested_If_Statement.rpt

Report Requirement: Demonstrate how nested If Statements work.

Report Details:

Table(s)	Fields
Product	Product Name Color Size Supplier_ID

1. Create a new multiple valued parameter called "prmColor" and set its default values to the content of the Color Field.

2. Create a new multiple valued parameter called "prmSize" and set the default values to the content of the Size field.

3. Create a new multiple valued parameter called "prmSupplier" and set the default values to the content of the Supplier Field.

4. In the Record Selection formula, enter the following code:

```
If {Product.Color} In {?prmcolor} Then
        True
Else If {Product.Size} In {?prmSize} Then
        True
Else If {Product.Supplier ID} In {?prmSupplier} Then
        True
Else
        False;
```

5. Refresh the report.

6. When prompted, select one or more values per parameter.

The report will display any record which matches with any of the three
fields with the three parameter's values.

NB: In an If Statement like the one above, as soon as a condition
resolves as True, the If Statement will stop evaluating. This has some
handy uses as we saw in the previous chapter.

7. In the Record Selection formula, delete all the code and enter
    the following:

```
If {Product.Color} = "Black" Then
(
        If {Product.Size} In {?prmSize} Then
                True
        Else If {Product.Supplier ID} In {?prmSupplier}
        Then
                True
        Else
                False;
)
Else
(
        False
);
```

8. Refresh the report.

9. When prompted, select one or more values per parameter.

The report will display any record that has "Black" in the Color Field and also matches with either of the two fields within the first set of brackets.

Alternatively…

10. In the Record Selection formula, delete all the existing code and enter the following:

```
If {Product.Color} = "Black" Then
(
        False;
)
Else
(
        If {Product.Size} In {?prmSize} Then
                True
        Else If {Product.Supplier ID} In {?prmSupplier}
        Then
                True
        Else
                False;
);
```

11. Refresh the report.

12. When prompted, select one or more values per parameter.

The report now does the exact opposite as before and shows the logic at work.

When to use Select Case

The Select Case Statement does nothing that a list of If Statements can not.

However, for ease of reading and later amendment, the Select Case is very useful.

To change the color of the Detail Section based on the customer's country, the following lesson uses the If Statement to determine the color used.

Report Name: select_Example.rpt

Report Requirement: Example of how a Select Case works.

Report Details:

Table(s)	Fields
Customer	CustomerID Customer Name City Country

1. Create a formula called "frmCountryByColor", and enter the following code:

```
If {Customer.Country} = "USA" Then
        crRed
Else If {Customer.Country} = "Canada" Then
        crBlue
Else If {Customer.Country} = "England" Then
        crGreen
Else If {Customer.Country} = "Australia" Then
        crGray
Else If {Customer.Country} = "Brazil" Then
        crYellow
```

```
        Else If {Customer.Country} = "France" Then
                crPurple
        Else
                crWhite;
```

2. Save and close the formula.

3. Insert the formula into the Detail Section.

4. Preview the report.

Note how the formula displays as a number field. This number relates to the color constants used in the formula.

5. Through the Section Expert, open the Color formula for the Detail Section and enter the following code:

```
        {@CountryByColor};
```

6. Save and close the formula.

7. Preview the report.

The Detail Section will change color based on the Country as dictated by the If Statement with a default of white if no Country matches.

The equivalent Select Case Statement does exactly the same job, but is in many ways 'cleaner':

8. Open the formula frmCountryByColor and delete the If Statement and replace it with the following:

```
        Select{Customer.Country}
        Case "USA":
                crRed
        Case "Canada":
                crBlue
        Case "England":
```

```
               crGreen
       Case  "Australia":
               crGray
       Case  "Brazil":
               crYellow
       Case "France":
               crPurple
       Default:
               crWhite;
```

9. Save and close the formula.

10. Preview the report.

The report with be exactly the same as before.

Just like If Statements, Select Statements can contain numerous statements in brackets like so:

```
       Select{Customer.Country}
       Case "USA":
           (
                   intTax := 15;
                   intShippingCost := 20;
           )
```

It is a matter of personal preference as to whether an If Statement or a Select Case is used.

Being aware of both is helpful, especially when modifying other developer's code. A lot of report writers, including myself, use both of these depending on how many different values need to be evaluated.

Personally, if less than four possible options are to be evaluated I will use an If Statement, more than that, a Select Case.

IIf, Switch and Choose.

I'm covering these three statements together. There are all quite useful, but seldom used, and it is certainly possible to write formulas without them.

However, they do come in handy occasionally, and it is useful to understand them in case they occur when amending another developer's work.

The IIf Statement is very similar to the If Statement in Excel, and for that reason, it does get used quite often by report writers who also work with spreadsheets.

1. Create a formula called "frmIIf_Formula" and enter the following code:

    ```
    IIf({Customer.Country} = "USA", crBlue, crBlack);
    ```

2. Save and close the formula.

3. Select all the fields in the Detail Section, and open the Font Color Formula Editor and enter the following code:

    ```
    {@IIF_Formula};
    ```

4. Save and close the formula.

5. Preview the report.

Any Customer based in the USA will now display in blue. Using the more common If Statement, it would look like this:

```
If ({Customer.Country} = "USA" Then
        crBlue
Else
        crBlack;
```

The first comma in the IIf Statement is the equivalent to the "Then" of the If Statement. The second comma is equal to the "Else".

IIf Statements can be nested just like their Excel counterparts:

6. Open the formula frmIfF_Formula and amend it to match the following:

```
IIf({Customer.Country} = "USA", crBlue,
IIf({Customer.Country} = "Canada", crRed, crBlack));
```

7. Save and close the formula.

8. Preview the report.

Canadian based customers now show with a red font.

The Switch Statement is somewhere between a Select Case and an If Statement and can be replaced by either.

It is, however, a rather elegant solution when dealing with 'bands' of criteria.

In the lesson below, the total sales from the year before are used to grade the company's customers.

1. Create a formula called "frmSwitch" and enter the following code:

```
Switch ({Customer.Last Year's Sales} > 100000, "Gold
Customer",
{Customer.Last Year's Sales} > 20000, "Silver Customer",
True, "Standard Customer");
```

2. Save and close the formula.

3. Insert the formula frmSwitch into the Details Section and preview the report.

The Switch Statement works in pairs, where a condition is associated with a result.

In the above lesson, Customer Sales over £100000 will provide the result of "Gold Customer" and if this condition is not true, the next condition is evaluated…and so on.

The If Statement equivalent of the above formula is:

```
If {Customer.Last Year's Sales} > 100000 Then
        "Gold Customer"
Else If {Customer.Last Year's Sales} > 20000 Then
        "Silver Customer"
Else
        "Standard Customer";
```

And finally, the Choose Function.

The Choose Function is also based on logical criteria, but is different enough from the If and Select Case Statements to be useful in it's own right.

The Choose Function is comprised of two parts:

4. A number which acts as an index to the second part.

5. A list of array items.

This function often used to be used to identify week days by name, but this has now been replaced by the WeekDayName Function. However, this serves as a good example as to how to use this function.

6. Create a formula called "frmChoose" and enter the following code:

Choose(DayOfWeek({Orders.Order Date}), "Sunday",
"Monday", "Tuesday", "Wednesday", "Thursday",
"Friday", "Saturday");

7. Save and close the formula.

8. Insert the formula into the Details Section and preview the
   report.

The correct day name will be displayed for each record.

This can also be used for naming quarters of the year or assigning a
team name to an ID field.

A Word on Formatting

Making formula code clear and easy to read is not a prerequisite for it to work.

But once you get past two lines of code, it can become very difficult to read / understand / amend formulas which are not formatted correctly.

Compare this:

```
If x = y Then
        "1"
Else If y = z Then
        "2"
Else If a = b Then
        "3"
Else
        "4";
```

To this:

If x = y Then "1" Else If y = z Then "2" Else If a = b Then "3" Else "4";

The Crystal Formula Editor will accept both, but first one is a lot easier to read and understand than the other.

There are four general rules to follow which will ensure that your formula code is easy to read:

1. Code dependant on Control Structures (If Statements, Select Case, etc) start on a new line.

2. A new command: a new line.

3. Indent by one tab for each branch of logic.

4. Insert a line between blocks of code doing similar things.

That this chunk of code as an example:

```
If x > y Then(Variable1 := 2; Variable2 := 3; Variable3 := 22;
Variable4 := 3; For Z := 1 To 5 Do (y := y + Z; y := y +
RecordCount;); Z;)Else(False;):
```

Step 1 alters the format to:

```
If x > y Then
(
Variable1 := 2; Variable2 := 3; Variable3 := 22; Variable4 := 3;
For Z := 1 To 5 Do
(
y := y + Z; y := y + RecordCount;
);
Z;
)
Else
(
False;
):
```

This step alone makes it a lot easier to read. Step 2 takes it a step
further by ensuring all commands are on separate lines:

```
If x > y Then
(
Variable1 := 2;
Variable2 := 3;
Variable3 := 22;
Variable4 := 3;
For Z := 1 To 5 Do
(
y := y + Z;
y := y + RecordCount;
);
Z;
```

```
)
Else
(
False;
):
```

Step three indents code to make it clear which lines are run together:

```
If x > y Then
(
        Variable1 := 2;
        Variable2 := 3;
        Variable3 := 22;
        Variable4 := 3;
        For Z := 1 To 5 Do
        (
                y := y + Z;
                y := y + RecordCount;
        );
        Z;
)
Else
(
        False;
):
```

And finally step four, which splits up code into logical chunks to make it clear which code lines are doing a similar job or are part of a logical sequence:

```
 If x > y Then
(
        Variable1 := 2;
        Variable2 := 3;
        Variable3 := 22;
        Variable4 := 3;

        For Z := 1 To 5 Do
```

```
              (
                    y := y + Z;
                    y := y + RecordCount;
              );

              Z;
      )
      Else
      (
              False;
      ):
```

The above formula code is obviously clearer and easier to read than the original block it is based on.

While this may seem like extra work, formatting formulas as you write them takes little extra effort. I personally tend to reformat other people's formulas while amending to make them more readable.

Loops

Loops are control structures which allow a formula to perform the same task numerous times. They work by evaluating a condition and then process one or more lines of code if the condition is False.

For example, loops can be used to interrogate a single text field several times, but are more normally used when dealing with arrays. Arrays are a subject in themselves, and are covered in depth in the **Arrays** Chapter, including how to use Loop Control structures with them.

The Difference Between While and For Loops

Two main types of Loops exist:

- While Loop
- For Loop

The While Loop will repeat itself until a particular condition becomes True. The For Loop repeats an action a certain number of times.

Using While Loops

There are two variations of the While Loop:

- While…Do
- Do…While

The difference between the two may seem slight, but can make a big different to formula results.

While…Do evaluates a condition, and if False it continues to process

The following exercise shows the usage of the For Loop and both variations of the While Loop.

Report Name: Loop_Examples.rpt

Report Requirement: Demonstrate the various uses and methods available for carrying out multiple data evaluations.

Report Details:

Table(s)	Fields
Product_Type	Product Type ID Product Type Name Description

1.　Create a new formula called "frmSpacesInStrFirstSentence".

2.　Enter the following code:

```
numberVar x := 1;
numberVar intNumberOfSpaces := 0;

While {Product_Type.Description}[x] <> "." Do
(
        If {Product_Type.Description}[x] = " " Then
                intNumberOfSpaces := intNumberOfSpaces
        + 1;

        x := x + 1;
);

intNumberOfSpaces;
```

3.　Save and close the formula.

4.　Insert the formula into the Detail Section.

5.　Preview the report.

The formula loops through each character in the Description Field until it reaches a "." which causes it to stop.

Within the loop, an If Statement identifies if the character is a space, and adds one to the number variable intNumberOfSpaces.

By the time the While Loop condition is met, intNumberOfSpaces contains the total number of spaces within the first sentence.

As intNumberOfSpaces is the last thing listed in the code, which is what is displayed.

If the same While Loop is used to extract the first sentence from the field:

6. Create a new formula called "frmStrFirstSentence".

7. Enter the following code:

```
numberVar y := 1;
stringVar strFirstSentence:= "";

While {Product_Type.Description}[y] <> "." Do
(
        strFirstSentence:= strFirstSentence &
        {Product_Type.Description}[y];

        y := y + 1;
);

strFirstSentence;
```

8. Save and close the formula.

9. Insert the formula into the Detail Section and preview the report.

The first sentence displayed is actually missing the full stop as the Loop stops processing when it hits the first full stop and so doesn't add the character to the variable strFirstSentence.

This could be corrected by adding a "." to the end of the variable after the loop:

```
strFirstSentence := strFirstSentence &  ".";
```

This will work with the current example, but that is not always the case.

For any loop that requires to evaluate on all the cycles of the loop, (including when the condition to end the loop is met) use the Do…While Loop:

10. Open the formula frmStrFirstSentence.

11. Replace the code with the following:

```
numberVar y := 0;
stringVar strFirstSentence:= "";

 Do
 (
        y := y + 1;

        strFirstSentence:= strFirstSentence &
        {Product_Type.Description}[y];

 )While {Product_Type.Description}[y] <> ".";

 strFirstSentence;
```

12. Save and close the formula.

13. Preview the report.

Because the Do…While Loop evaluates the code before it checks the While condition, the last digit (a "." In this case) is included.

Both the While…Do and Do…While Loops will loop a varying amount of times depending on the condition set.

When there is a need to loop through something the same amount of times, every time, use the For Loop:

14. Create a new formula called "frmListVowels".

15. Enter the following code:

```
numberVar z;
stringVar strVowelList := "";

For z := 1 To 20 Do
(
        If {Product_Type.Description}[z] in
        ["a","e","i","o","u"] Then
        (
                strVowelList := strVowelList &
                {Product_Type.Description}[z];
        );
);

strVowelList;
```

16. Save and close the formula.

17. Insert the formula into the Detail Section and preview the report.

NB: The variable used to increment from 1 to 20 (in this exercise) will do so automatically, unlike in the While Loops and does not need to be explicity written in the formula code.

The For Loop loops twenty times through the code in the brackets. When the If Statement evaluates as true, the character being referenced is appended to the variable strVowelList.

NB: Occasionally, there is a need to *not* run the code within a Loop every time. The data itself may increase in greater amounts than one (Example: sales for a specific week day), or the report may only be interested in a subset of the data being looked at (example: every fourth week).

The For Loop also comes with a handy Step option which enables the Loop to increment in greater amounts than 1:

18. Open the formula called frmListVowels.

19. Alter the For Statement to the following:

```
numberVar z;
stringVar strVowelList := "";

For z := 1 To 20 Step 2 Do
(
        If {Product_Type.Description}[z] in
        ["a","e","i","o","u"] Then
        (
                strVowelList := strVowelList &
                {Product_Type.Description}[z]
        );
);

strVowelList;
```

20. Save and close the formula.

21. Preview the report.

With the Step option added, the For Loop increments in multiples of 2.

NB: a Step of -1 will cause the For Loop to count backwards.

A common problem with For Loops arises when the maximum increment number is greater than needed to evaluate the code:

22. Create a new formula called "frmFirst10Vowels".

23. Enter the following code:

```
numberVar z;
stringVar strVowelList := "";

For z := 1 To 200000 Do
(
        If {Product_Type.Description}[z] in
        ["a","e","i","o","u"] Then
        (
                strVowelList := strVowelList &
                {Product_Type.Description}[z];
        );
);

strVowelList;
```

24. Save and close the formula.

25. Insert the formula into the Detail Section and preview the report.

The report will error as 200,000 is greater than the length of some of the fields the For Loop is looking at.

In some cases this is a sign that the wrong type of loop is being used and a While Loop should be considered.

However, the Exit For command allows the For Loop to be broken before reaching the end of its limit (in this case 200,000).

26. Open the formula called frmFirst10Vowels.

27. Replacing the existing code with the following:

```
numberVar z;
stringVar strVowelList := "";

For z := 1 To 200000  Do
(
        If Len({Product_Type.Description}) < z Then
                Exit For;

        If {Product_Type.Description}[z] in
        ["a","e","i","o","u"] Then
        (
                strVowelList := strVowelList &
                {Product_Type.Description}[z]
        );
);

strVowelList;
```

28. Save and close the formula.

29. Preview the report.

An Exit While exists for While Loops and can be added as a safe guard against a While Loop never reaching a completed condition to finish.

30. Create a new formula called "frmLettersUpToK".

31. Enter the following code:

```
numberVar v := 1;
stringVar strLettersUpToK:= "";

While {Product_Type.Description}[v] <> "k" Do
(
```

```
            strLettersUpToK:= strLettersUpToK &
            {Product_Type.Description}[v];

            v := v + 1;
        );

        strLettersUpToK;
```

32. Save and close the formula.

33. Insert the formula into the Detail Section and preview the report.

The formula will error as many of the Description Fields do not contain the letter "k" so the While Loop will try to run forever.

NB: In this exercise the formula errors once the variable 'v' is greater than the length of the Description Field, however, it is possible to have loops which can run forever (or at least, reach Crystal Reports set limits).

34. Open the formula called frmLettersUpToK.

35. Amend the existing code to the following:

```
        numberVar v := 1;
        stringVar strLettersUpToK:= "";

        While {Product_Type.Description}[v] <> "k" Do
        (

            strLettersUpToK := strLettersUpToK &
            {Product_Type.Description}[v];

            v := v + 1;

            If v > Len({Product_Type.Description}) Then
                Exit While;
        );
```

strLettersUpToK;

36. Save and close the formula.

37. Preview the report.

In a manner similar to the For Loop in the previous exercise, the While Loop exits once the variable 'v' becomes greater than the length of the Description Field, unless the character "k" is encountered and the loop ends naturally.

Arrays

An Explanation of Arrays

Arrays are variations on the basic variable types and allow some very complex formulas to be created quite easily.

An array is a variable which can hold numerous values at once which can be accessed via an index.

It may help to think of how a column in a spreadsheet can hold lots of different values identified by their row numbers.

	A
1	James
2	Paul
3	Neil
4	David
5	Steve

A1 would reference "James" in the above spreadsheet.

A number in [] denotes which 'row' the data is stored in, so the equivalent to A1 in Crystal Reports is:

```
arstrFirstName[1];
```

Adding a value to an array is the same as with a normal variable, but with the addition of the index number:

```
arstrFirstName[1] := "Zhenya";
```

When combined with Loop Functions arrays are very powerful.

A string is an array in its own right, and is just a collection (or 'string') of single characters.

                {Employee.First Name} [1];

Returns the first letter of {Employee.First Name}.

NB: Crystal Reports starts counting at 1, and not 0 like most other programming languages.

This is a little more simple than:

                Mid({Employee.First Name },1,1);

To declare an array:

```
stringVar array astrWeekDays := ["Sunday","Monday",
"Tuesday",...];

astrWeekDays(DayOfWeek({Orders.Order Date}));
```

First the array is created, then the DayOfWeek Function used to pick one of the array elements.

Alternatively use if you only plan on using it once:

```
Choose(DayOfWeek({Orders.Order Date}),"Sunday","Monday",
"Tuesday",...);
```

To add values to an array during a formula, declare it with a number for the amount of elements for the array:

```
stringVar array x := [" "];
numberVar y;

For y := 1 To 50  Do
(
        Redim x [UBound(x)+1];
```

```
        );

        UBound(x);
```

UBound returns the number of elements in the array, adding one to that number and using Redim extends the array.

Using the above formula will delete the contents of the array every time it is 'Redim'ed. Use the 'Preserve' keyword to keep the contents and resize the array:

```
        stringVar array x := [" "];
        numberVar y;

        For y := 1 To 50  Do
        (
                Redim Preserve x [UBound (x)+1];
        );

        UBound(x);
```

'UBound' returns the highest element number. 'Minimum' and 'Maximum' get the contents of lowest and highest elements. The 'Maximum' is useful for displaying the top end of a range, but as the minimum is always 1: the 'Minimum' is not much use.

Using Arrays

The following lessons take you step by step through all of the array related functions discussed in the previous section.

This is probably the most difficult area of formulas for non-programmers to grasp, but once arrays are mastered they are a very useful tool to have.

Report Name: Array_Usage.rpt

Report Requirement: The requirement is to count all the employees for each country in the Report Footer of a report which is grouped by employee position.

Without arrays this could only be realised by subreport.

Report Details:

Table(s)	Fields	Group(s)
Employee	Employee ID Last Name First Name Position	Position
Employee_Addresses	City Region Country	

Creating arrays

First, the array variables must be declared to hold the country, and another one to hold the number of employees.

1. Create a formula called "frmUpdatearray" and add the following code:

```
stringVar array astrCountry;
numberVar array aintStaffTotal;
```

The array variables need to be populated for each record returned.

2. Add the following declarations to hold numbers for looping through the array:

```
Local numberVar x;
Local numberVar y;
```

3. An If Statement is used to identify whether each Country is already listed in the array "astrCountry":

```
If {Employee_Addresses.Country} In astrCountry Then
(
```

4. If the country is in the astrCountry array, the formula finds which element of the array is holding it by looping through the whole array and recording the index in variable "y":

```
For x:=1 To UBound(astrCountry)  Do
(
        If {Employee_Addresses.Country} =
        astrCountry[x] Then
                y:=x;
);
```

5. The variable "y" is then used to identify the correct element of the aintStaffTotal array to add an employee to:

```
aintStaffTotal[y] := aintStaffTotal[y] + 1;
)
```

6. However, if the country is not already in astrCountry, a new array element must be created so it can be added, as well as a new element in the array aintStaffTotal to hold the Staff Total:

```
        Else
        (
                Redim Preserve
                astrCountry[UBound(astrCountry)+1];
                Redim Preserve
                aintStaffTotal[UBound(aintStaffTotal)+1];
```

7. With the new elements created, the country can be added to astrCountry and the first employee can be counted and added to the aintStaffTotal:

```
                astrCountry[UBound(astrCountry)] :=
                {Employee_Addresses.Country};
                aintStaffTotal[UBound(aintStaffTotal)] := 1;
        );
```

8. Save and close the formula.

9. Insert the formula in the Detail Section and suppress it.

With this formula, the report will build two arrays, one for the country, and one to hold the total number of employees located within that country.

As arrays have been created and expanded in unison, the Country and the Staff Total will match when indexed.

Accessing Arrays

To display the two arrays we are going to create two different (but similar) formulas, one for each.

1. Create a formula called "frmDisplayCountryarray" and add the following code to ensure it only runs after the frmUpdatearray formula has populated the arrays:

> EvaluateAfter ({@frmUpdatearray});

2. Add the array variable so we can access it's contents, and a number variable to count through the array:

    ```
    stringVar array astrCountry;
    numberVar z;
    ```

3. Add a string variable to hold the list of countries, and add the column heading to the array:

    ```
    stringVar strDisplayCountry;
    astrCountry[1] := "Country" & Chr(13);
    ```

4. Loop through every array element (omitting the first as it is empty) and add them to the variable strDisplayCountry:

    ```
    For z := 1 To UBound(astrCountry) Do
    (
            strDisplayCountry := strDisplayCountry &
            astrCountry[z] & Chr(13);
    );
    ```

5. Finally, display the contents of the string variable:

    ```
    strDisplayCountry;
    ```

6. Save and close the formula.

7. Insert the formula in the Report Footer Section.

8. Enable the "Can Grow" option.

9. Preview the report.

The formula lists all the Countries which appear in the report.

The Chr(13) ensures a new line is started after each country.

The second formula is so similar that it is not given the same step by step breakdown:

10. Create a formula called "frmDisplayStaffTotalarray" and add the following code:

```
EvaluateAfter ({@frmUpdatearray});

numberVar array aintStaffTotal;

numberVar t;

stringVar strDisplayStaff;
aintStaffTotal[1] := "Number Of Staff" & Chr(13);

For t := 1 To UBound(aintStaffTotal) Do
(
        strDisplayStaff := strDisplayStaff &
        ToText(aintStaffTotal[t],0,"") & Chr(13);
);

strDisplayStaff;
```

11. Save and close the formula.

12. Insert the formula next to, and aligned with frmDisplayCountryarray.

13. Enable the "Can Grow" option.

14. Preview the report.

The report now contains detail level data grouped by position, and a summary list of countries showing how many employees live in each, in the Report Footer.

Without arrays this would only be possible with a subreport.

Arrays are an involved subject, and more examples are provided in Sections Two and Three of this book.

Ranges

Ranges are a type of array, but rather than being lists of values they just contain a start and end value.

So an array like this:

    aintarray := [1, 2, 3, 4, 5, 6, 7, 8, 9, 10, 11, 12, 13, 14, 15, 16];

Can be created as a range like this:

    rintRange := [1 To 16];

Ranges are particularly useful when used to represent a series of dates:

    rdteRange := [#15/01/2009# To #15/01/2010#];

Ranges are commonly used in parameters, but have a variety of other uses.

All the functions discussed for arrays are valid for use with ranges.

Report Name: Range_Examples.rpt

Report Requirement: In the following tutorial, the report has to be filtered on a date range parameter and list an abridged position of each employee.

Report Details:

Table(s)	Fields
Employee	Employee ID Last Name First Name Position Hire Date

1. Create a new date parameter called "prmHireDateSelection" and check the option for Range.

2. Save and close the parameter and insert into the Report Header Section.

3. Preview the report and enter a start and end date in the parameter when prompted.

The parameter shows as blank as it contains numerous values and does not know which to display.

Including a range in a report title is not a straight forward case of drag and drop.

4. Create a new formula called "frmDateTitleRange" and enter the following code:

```
"Hired From " & Minimum({?prmHireDateSelection }) & " 
To " & Maximum({?prmHireDateSelection });
```

5. Save and close the formula.

6. Insert the formula into the Report Header Section and preview the report.

The formula may need resizing, and will display the two dates entered.

NB: When entering a range in a parameter there is an option to have "No Lower Value" or "No Upper Value" limits. If these options are selected they will be blank in the above formula.

The report is quite misleading at the moment, as its title suggests the data is filtered, when currently it is not.

7. Open the Formula Editor for Record Selection and enter the following code:

```
        If {Employee.Hire Date} In {?prmHireDateSelection} Then
                True
        Else
                False;
```

8. Save and close the formula.

9. Refresh the report several times and enter various date values when prompted

The report will now show data which matches the dates in the title.

Now, all that remains is to abbreviate the employee's job title.

10. Create a new formula called "frmPositionAbbreviation" and enter the following code:

```
        {Employee.Position}[1 To 9];
```

11. Save and close the formula.

12. Insert the formula in the Detail Section and preview the report.

The position field is edited to only show the first nine characters.

This is the basic usage of arrays and ranges, but they are covered repeatedly in other chapters of this book in their myriad of practical applications.

Handling Nulls

Nulls are essentially nothing, but can cause a lot of problems when writing formulas and produce inaccurate results. Nulls get into reports from database fields which are empty and can be created within a report via formulas that don't equate to anything:

```
If 2=3 then
        "yes";
```

Nulls cannot be assigned manually to a variable.

Nulls are not equal to other nulls in the way that 1 = 1 or "a" = "a".

To test for a Null value:

```
If IsNull({Employee.Position }) = True then
(
        "Field is Null"
)
Else
(
        "Field is not Null"
);
```

From the Options Menu a default value for Nulls can be set. This is not advised as fields may use the default value you choose to replace the Null with.

Using IsNull

Nulls can not be added or concatenated and will turn the whole formula into a Null, so be sure to test for them If you are in any doubt:

```
stringVar strFirstName := " ";
stringVar strLastName := " ";
```

```
If isnull({Customer.First Name}) = false then
(
        strFirstName := {Customer.First Name};
);

If isnull({Customer.Last Name}) = false then
(
        strLastName := {Customer.Last Name};
);

strFirstName & " " & strLastName;
```

This code is used to check that a database field does not contain a Null before trying to add it to the string variables.

Record Selection with Formulas

Beyond the Select Expert

Most of the basic requirements for limiting the information being displayed in a report can be met via the Select Expert. And while some moderately complex filters can be built solely using the Select Expert, a greater level of control can be created by using formulas to limit which records are used in a report.

The way the Select Expert actually works is by creating a formula based on the options selected.

The selection formula is a boolean, and so only returns True or False to determine whether or not a record from a database is included in the report.

Two types of selection formula exist in versions of Crystal Reports prior to 2008:

- Record
- Group

Both work in similar ways, but are evaluated at different times. In the case of Group Record selection this can cause numerous problems with data in reports.

Record selection formula is calculated as the report interrogates the database. If a record does not match the criteria, the report does not include it.

The Group Selection formula is based on the results of Group Summaries, and so can only be evaluated once the report has calculated the groups. Therefore, all records are included in the report and will show in chart, cross-tabs and summary totals, even though they are hidden and apparently filtered.

This problem can be overcome using Running Totals, which are dicussed at length in the Chapter **Running Totals**.

From the Crystal Reports 2008 release onwards there is a third option:

- Saved

This third option is identical to the Record Selection option but is only applied to reports which have data saved with them.

This is particularly useful when working offsite or distributing reports via the Crystal Reports Viewer and allows users to further filter report without connection to the database.

All three of these filtering types can be used together.

Report Name: selection_Formula.rpt

Report Requirement: : This exercise consists of creating a filter which limits the records displayed in the report by the value of the customer's Last Year's Sales.

However, different countries (as selected by the user) need different levels of Sales to be included.

Country	Last Year's Sales Minimum
USA	65000
England	50000
France	45000
Germany	35000
Everywhere Else	30000

Implementing the logic to realise the above is impossible using only the selection Expert.

Report Details:

Table(s)	Fields
Customer	Customer ID Address1 Address2 City Postal Code Last Year's Sales

The first step is limiting the country based on a parameter using the Select Expert, to show how the Select Expert ties into the Record Selection formula.

1. Create a string parameter called "prmOneOrMoreCountry" allowing multiple values, with a default list of values based on the Country Field.

2. Open the Select Expert and set Country 'is equal to' {?prmOneOrMoreCountry}.

3. Click on the 'Show formula' button to view the formula created by the Select Expert:

    {Customer.Country} = {?prmOneOrMoreCountry}

4. In the Report Menu, pick 'Selection formulas', then 'Record…' to open the Record Selection Formula Editor.

NB: The code panel already contains the code created by the Select Expert.

5. Amend the code to include a Select Case Statement:

    {Customer.Country} In {?prmOneOrMoreCountry}
    And
    Select {Customer.Country}
    Case "USA":

```
                {Customer.Last Year's Sales} > 65000
        Case "England":
                {Customer.Last Year's Sales} > 50000
        Case "France":
                {Customer.Last Year's Sales} > 45000
        Case "Germany":
                {Customer.Last Year's Sales} > 35000
        Default:
                {Customer.Last Year's Sales} > 30000;
```

6. Save and close the formula.

7. Preview the report.

Refresh the report a few times with different countries selected.

The formula first evaluates whether the country is the same as any selected in the parameter {?prmOneOrMoreCountry}. If there is a match, the Select Case Statement is evaluated and compares the 'Last Year's Sales' to a minimum value, which If it is greater, will return True and the record will be accepted into the report.

This formula is run for each row of data as it is read by the report.

Group Filters

Group Filters are underused in Crystal Reports, but are very powerful when used properly and in conjunction with running totals.

Group Filters limit record selection based on Summary Operations, like Sum or Count etc.,so are ideal for any report which needs to display only employees with more than twelve sick days or orders which have a total value of under £10000.

Report Name: Group_Selection.rpt

Report Requirement: Display customers whose orders are greater in value than they placed last year, and who have also made at least half that amount in payments.

Report Details:

Table(s)	Fields	Group(s)
Customer	Customer Name Last Year's Sales	Customer_ID
Orders	Order_ID Order Amount Payment Received	

Conveniently, last years sales have already been totalled, and the result is held in the Customer table.

For current sales, the Order Amount must be added together for each customer.

1. Insert a Sum Summary based on the field 'Order Amount' and grouped by Customer ID.

2. Insert a Sum Summary based on the field 'Order Amount' grouped on the whole report.

3. Preview the report.

Totals now appear in the Group Footer Section and at the end of the report.

Make a note of the grand total.

4. Open the Group selection Formula Editor (via the Report Menu—Selection formulas) and enter the following code:

```
Sum ({Orders.Order Amount}, {Customer.Customer ID}) >
{Customer.Last Year's Sales};
```

5. Save and close the formula, and refresh the report.

The report now limits the data displayed to customers who have ordered more this year than last.

Check the value in the grand total.

It has not changed, despite less data being shown in the report.

Because a Group Filter can only be calculated after all the records have been read into the report, all totals are generated before the filtering is done.

NB: This is one of the few times that Crystal Reports can be considered to 'make a mistake'.

The easiest way to correct the summary errors is to use running totals with the same criteria as the Group Selection formula. This is covered in detail in the Chapter **Running Totals**.

6. Re-open the Group Formula Editor, and amend the code by adding the following beneath the existing condition:

```
And
Sum ({Orders.Order Amount}, {Customer.Customer ID}) <
10000;
```

7. Save and close the formula.

8. Preview the report.

The grand total still shows the original value.

9. Re-open the Group Formula Editor, and copy the code. Close the formula.

10. Create a Running Total based on the Ordered Amount. Select the Evaluate option of "use a formula" and paste the code from the Group Selection.

11. Close the Running Total and drag it into the Report Footer.

12. Preview the report.

The Running Total displays the correct result.

As this exercise highlights - always use Running Totals with Group Filters.

Complex Conditional Filtering

The beauty of using formulas to create record filters, as opposed to the Select Expert, is that an extreme level of complexity and control can be reached.

A particular advantage of this is the ability to make parameters optional when running the report, thus giving the user the choice of how to filter the report.

There are two methods of achieving this. From Crystal Reports 2008 onwards there are specific methods available for handling optional parameters, which will be covered later in this chapter.

First though, the formula work around which was needed before Crystal Reports 2008.

The two methods are very similar, but the following lesson is worth undertaking regardless of which version of Crystal Reports being used as it provides an example of how to manipulate filters.

Report Name: Optional_Parameters_Old.rpt

Report Requirement: Create a report which displays a list of customers and their business address.

The user has to have the option to filter on one or more of the following:

- Country

- A word that appears in the Company Name.

- Last Year's Sales over a certain amount.

Report Details:

Table(s)	Fields
Customer	Customer Name Address1 Address2 City Country Postal Code

1. Create a string parameter called "prmSelectCountry" which accepts multiple values and has a default list based on the Country Field.

2. Add " NONE" as an option to the default list (take care to include the leading space) and order the parameter to display the list in alphabetical order.

3. Save and close the parameter.

4. Create a string parameter called "prmSelectWord" which accepts a single value and has a default of " NONE" (again, take care to include the leading space).

5. Save and close the parameter.

6. Create a string parameter called "prmSelectSalesAmount" which accepts a single value and has a default of " NONE".

7. Save and close the parameter.

If we were limited to using the Select Expert, we would have to choose which to include in the filter now while developing the report and the user would have no choice in which parameters to ignore.

But now, between the " NONE" default value and the Record Selection formula, the user can select which, if any, parameters to use.

8. Open the Record Selection Formula Editor and declare the following variable to hold whether or not a particular record will be included in the report:

> booleanVar blnInclude_Record := False;

9. Add an If Statement to check if the user has made any selections to filter the report by country. If not, include the record, if they have, compare the Country Field to the user selection:

> If {?prmSelectCountry} = " NONE" Then
>   blnInclude_Record := True
> Else
>   blnInclude_Record := ({Customer.Country} In
>   {?prmSelectCountry});

10. After the above If Statement blnInclude_Record will be True if the user has decided not to filter on country or has picked a country which matches the record. It will only be False if the user has filter on a country(s) and it has not matched.

    So if the filter has failed to match on this first step, it doesn't matter if it matches with any others.

    Add an If Statement to check for this possibility:

> If blnInclude_Record := False Then
>   False

11. Obviously, if the blnInclude_Record Variable is True, we need to check if the user wants to check against a word in the Customer Name. If they don't, the record is still acceptable for the report:

> Else If {?Select_Word} = " NONE" Then
>   blnInclude_Record := True

12. If the user has entered a value to find in the Customer Name, we need to compare it to the Customer Name and place the result in blnInclude_Record:

```
Else
        blnInclude_Record := ({Customer.Customer Name}
        LIKE "*" & {?Select_Word} & "*");
```

BlnInclude_Record will be True if the user has selected either values that match their respective fields or chosen " NONE".

So, If blnInclude_Record is False it means the record has failed and does not need to be compared to the third criteria.

13. Add an If Statement to check for this possibility:

```
If blnInclude_Record := False Then
        False
```

Obviously, if the blnInclude_Record variable is True, we need to check if the user wants to check against a word in the Customer Name.

14. If they don't, the record is still acceptable for the report:

```
Else If {?prmSelectWord} = " NONE" Then
        blnInclude_Record := True
```

15. If the user has entered a value to find in the Customer Name, we need to compare it to the Customer Name and place the result in blnInclude_Record:

```
Else
        blnInclude_Record := ({Customer.Customer Name}
        LIKE "*" & {?Select_Word} & "*");
```

16. Finally, add the blnInclude_Record at the end of the formula to ensure that is the value returned:

blnInclude_Record;

17. Save and close the formula.

18. Preview the report several times trying different combinations of parameter values.

The formula works by testing each condition and storing the result in blnInclude_Record until one fails, then ignoring all subsequent comparisons.

By repeating the format of the second or third If Statement it is possible to expand the formula to include any number of extra parameters.

This lesson was a bit more involved than most of the formula presented in this section of the book, but it does highlight how the limitations of the Selection Expert can be overcome.

This next exercise will only work with versions of Crystal Reports 2008 onwards and illustrates how helpful the improved functionality is.

Report Name: Optional_Parameters.rpt

Report Requirement: This lesson is identical to the last in regard to the requirements to highlight the differences between the two methods.

Like the previous excerise, the user has to have the option to filter on one or more of the following:

- Country

- A word that appears in the Company Name.

- Last Year's Sales over a certain amount.

Report Details:

Table(s)	Fields
Customer	Customer Name Address1 Address2 City Country Postal Code

1. Create a string parameter called "prmSelectCountry" which accepts multiple values and has a default list based on the Country Field.

2. Add change the Optional Prompt value to True. Save and close the parameter.

3. Create a string parameter called "prmSelectWord" which accepts a single value and has Optional Prompt value set to True.

4. Create a number parameter called "prmSelectSalesAmount" which accepts a single value and a True Optional Prompt value.

5. Using the Select Expert, set the Country Field to be 'one of' the prmSelectCountry Parameter.

Open the Record Selection Formula Editor. The Select Expert has generated the following code:

```
(not HasValue({?prmSelectCountry}) Or
{Customer.Country} In [{?prmSelectCountry}])
```

This effectively replaces the If Statements used in the previous exercise.

6. Using the Select Expert, set the Last Year's Sales field to be 'Greater Than' the select_Sales_Amount parameter.

7. Open the Record Selection Formula Editor and add the following to the end of the existing (Select Expert generated) code:

```
and
(not HasValue({?prmSelectWord}) Or
{Customer.Customer Name} like "*" & {?prmSelectWord}
& "*")
```

8. Preview the report several times trying different combinations of parameter values.

Obviously this is the more elegant solution if the version of Crystal Reports in use supports it. But does require some extra work if any of the parameters are used in formulas within the report.

9. Create a new formula called "frmTitleOrderAmountMinimum" and add the following code:

```
{?Select_Sales_Amount};
```

10. Save and close the formula, and insert it into the Report Header Section.

11. Preview the report without selecting any value for the prmSelectSalesAmount parameter.

The instant the Preview Tab is clicked, the following error message is displayed:

"Parameter Has No Value"

To avoid this, the possibility of an optional parameter not having a value must be coded for every time it is used.

12. Open the formula called frmTitleOrderAmountMinimum and add the following code:

```
If HasValue({?prmSelectSalesAmount}) Then
        ToText({?prmSelectSalesAmount})
Else
        "No Minimum Price selected";
```

13. Save and close the formula.

14. Preview the report without selecting any value for the prmSelectSalesAmount Parameter.

This time there is no error message, and the text: "No Minimum Price selected" is displayed on the report.

Refresh the report a few times using different parameter options.

Performance Concerns regarding Record Selection

It should be clear by now that exceptionally complex Record Selection formulas are possible.

In instances where performance is an issue, special consideration should be given to complexity used to filter the data.

Ideally, any record selection should take place on the database server and a minimum of data transported over the network to Crystal Reports.

In the case of Group Selections, all the records are passed to Crystal Reports to generate the Group(s) and Summaries and determine which records should be included. When using large data sets and / or weak networks, this can cause slow reports.

When performance becomes a big issue due, use SQL procedures on the server to filter down the data and base the report on the results.

Drilldown Reports and Formulas

Drilldown reports provide a very powerful method for data analysis and allow the user to investigate the data behind the summarised totals in a report.

The problem with drilldown reports is that they quickly become messy when the formatting intended for the summary does not apply to the detailed data being revealed.

Report Name: DrillDown.rpt

Report Requirement: Create a report which allows managers to view Order Amounts by Country, and drill down to view the same summary by Region, City and Customer.

Report Details:

Table(s)	Fields	Group
Customer	Customer ID	Country Region City Customer
Order	Order ID Order Date Order Amount	

Additional Report Setup:

Insert a Sum summary based on the Order Amount for each group and place it in the Group Header.

Suppress all the Group Footer Sections.

Set Group Headers Sections 2 to 4 and the Details Section to "Hide (Drilldown OK)".

Delete all the title textboxes.

NB: Ensure that "Show All Headers On Drill Down" is ticked in the Report Options window.

The first step is to create a formula to display the current drilldown level for reference while developing the report.

1. Create a formula called "frmDrillLevelReference" and enter the following code:

   ```
   DrillDownGroupLevel;
   ```

2. Save and close the formula and add it to Page Header Section.

This formula will show which level is currently being viewed, which can be invaluable when becoming familiar with drilldown or when working on reports with lots of levels.

The next step is to only show the expanded Group Header and the listed Group Header beneath it.

3. Open the Section Expert for Group Header 1 and enter the following code for the Suppress formula:

   ```
   DrillDownGroupLevel > 1;
   ```

4. Save and close the formula, then highlight Group Header 2 and enter the following code for the Suppress formula:

   ```
   DrillDownGroupLevel > 2;
   ```

5. Save and close the formula, then highlight Group Header 3 and enter the following code for the Suppress formula:

   ```
   DrillDownGroupLevel > 3;
   ```

6. Save and close the formula and close the Section Expert.

7. Preview the report.

Drill down on each group until the Detail Section is displayed.

Select a Country like England, USA or Canada which have numerous orders and show the true value of the drilldown report.

On each successive drilldown, only the immediate group above is displayed.

So that the main group on each level of drilldown stands out more than the group listed beneath, the font style will be changed to bold.

8. Select both the fields in Group Header 2, right click and select "Format Field" and the Font Tab.

9. Under the formula icon for Style, enter the following code:

```
If DrillDownGroupLevel = 2 Then
        crBold
Else
        crRegular;
```

10. Save and close the formula.

11. Select both the fields in Group Header 3, right click and select "Format Field" and the Font Tab.

12. Under the formula icon for Style, enter the following code:

```
If DrillDownGroupLevel = 3 Then
        crBold
Else
        crRegular;
```

13. Save and close the formula.

14. Select both the fields in Group Header 4, right click and select "Format Field" and the Font Tab.

15. Under the formula icon for Style, enter the following code:

```
If DrillDownGroupLevel = 4 Then
        crBold
Else
        crRegular;
```

16. Save and close the formula.

17. Preview the report.

Drill down on each group until the Detail Section is displayed. At each level of drilldown, the main group is displayed with bold text and the listed group is shown with a regular font format.

The final step is to create meaningful titles for each column on the report, regardless of which level of drilldown in which it resides.

For the Group Name title field, a formula is needed that names the field that is the basis of the main group and type of field being listed as the child group.

18. Add a textbox in the Page Header Section above the Order Amount summary with the text:

    "Order Amount Total"

19. Add three textboxes in the Page Header Section, one for each of Customer ID, Order ID and Order Date.

20. Align the three textboxes above their respective fields, select all three textboxes and enter the following code for the Suppress formula:

```
If DrillDownGroupLevel <> 4 Then
        True
Else
        False;
```

21. Save and close the formula.

22. Create a new formula called "frmGroupNameTitle" and enter the following code:

```
Select DrillDownGroupLevel
Case 0:
        "Country"
Case 1:
        {Customer.Country} & " Regions"
Case 2:
        {Customer.Region} & " Cities"
Case 3:
        {Customer.City} & " Customers"
Case 4:
        "Customers";
```

23. Save and close the formula then insert it into the Page Header Section above the Group Names field.

24. Preview the report.

Drill down on each group until the Detail Section is displayed.

The report is now dynamically formatted in a way suitable for every level of drilldown.

Formulas and Summaries

For the most part, the previous exercises have focused on using formulas to manipulate individual fields or properties. But most formulas can be summarised like any other database field.

In addition to this, Crystal Reports provides a summary operation specific for use with formulas in the form of Running Totals.

NB: Running Totals used in conjunction with formulas are a powerful, yet greatly underused feature within Crystal Reports which can meet a variety of requirements that it would otherwise be difficult to realise.

Running Totals

Running Totals are the only way to provide summary information on reports filtered on Group selection formula.

The other main use for Running Totals is for conditional summaries (equivalent to the Countif Function in Excel) which allow an individual field to be evaluated by a formula in a similar way to record selection to determine if it is included in a summary.

Report Name: Summaries.rpt

Report Requirement: Display the total value of all orders under £100 by Customer.

Report Details:

Table(s)	Fields	Group(s)
Orders	Customer_ID Order_ID Order_Amount Payment_Received	Customer_ID

1. Create a new Running Total based on a Sum of the "Order Amount".

2. In the Evaluate Section, check the "use a formula" and open the associated Formula Editor.

3. The code needed to limit the records used in the Sum is the same as if filtering the report to only include "Order Amount" less than £100:

```
If {Orders.Order Amount} < 100 Then
        True
Else
        False;
```

4. In the Reset Section, check the option "On change of group".

5. Save and close the Running Total. Move the Running Total to the Group Footer.

6. Preview the report.

The report will now display the total of sales under £100 for each customer as each Order Amount is evaluated before being added.

A Running Total's evaluation does not have to be based on the field it is summarising.

The next stage is to add a Sum of all Order Amounts that have not been paid:

7. Create a new Running Total based on a Sum of the "Order Amount".

8. In the Evaluate Section, check the "use a formula" and open the associated Formula Editor.

9. This time, only include "Order Amount" when payment has not been received:

```
If {Orders.Payment Received} = False Then
        True
Else
        False;
```

10. In the Reset Section, check the option "On change of group".

11. Save and close the Running Total. Move the Running Total to the Group Footer.

12. Preview the report.

The new Running Total is only evaluated when the Payment Received Field is False.

Referencing a Summary

When a summary is used in Crystal Reports, it actually creates a small formula, much in the same way that a report writer would.

This can be then accessed from within other formulas or new summaries can be written by hand.

The next part of the exercise is to add a handling charge of 5% to the Order Amount totals.

13. If the report doesn't already have one, insert a Sum Summary based on the Order Amount Field.

14. Create a new formula called "frmHandlingCharge".

15. Scroll through the Report Fields Panel until you find the following:

    Group #1: Orders.Customer ID – A:Sum of Orders.Order Amount

16. Then double click (or drag and drop) it into the Code Panel:

    Sum ({Orders.Order Amount}, {Orders.Customer ID})

17. Increase the total by 5% by amending the code to the following:

    (ToNumber(Sum({Orders.Order Amount}, {Orders.Customer ID}))/100)* 5;

18. Save and close the formula, then insert into the Group 1 Footer.

19. Preview the report.

The report now shows the additional 5% Handling Charge.

The final step is to add it to the Order Amount Total to show the complete cost.

20. Open the formula frmHandlingCharge, wrap the origin code in bracket, then add the Sum to it:

    ((ToNumber(Sum({Orders.Order Amount}, {Orders.Customer ID})) /100)* 5) + Sum({Orders.Order Amount}, {Orders.Customer ID});

21. Save and close the formula.

22. Preview the report.

The combined total is now displayed.

Different types of summaries can be mixed and matched to good effect.

Summarising a Formula

Formulas can be summarised in the same way as database fields, but in most cases the same results can be achieved in a cleaner way using Running Totals.

The following lesson is included for completeness, and is useful when amending other developer's reports and the occasional situation when Running Totals are not enough.

The following lesson gives a simple example of how summarising a formula works by totalling the orders which have not been paid.

23. Create a new formula called "frmOwedOrderAmounts" and enter the following code:

```
If {Orders.Payment Received} = False Then
        {Orders.Order Amount}
Else
        0;
```

24. Save and close the formula.

25. Insert the formula into the Detail Section and preview the report.

The new formula will either display £0 if the order has been paid for, or the full value if it is outstanding.

Now, all that remains is to Sum the value.

26. Right click on the formula frmOwedOrderAmount and insert a Sum Summary based on Group 1.

27. Preview the report.

The Summary displays the outstanding balance for each customer.

Correct Formula Order

Why Correct Formulas Sometimes Error

It is possible for formulas which reference other formulas to produce erroneous results despite being correct in their own right.

This happens because formulas are not necessarily evaluated by Crystal Reports in the order necessary to get the expected results.

Controlling Execution Order

When a formula is evaluated it can be controlled with three functions that appear under the "Evaluation Time" folder:

- BeforeReadingRecords
- WhilePrintingRecords
- WhileReadingRecords

These dictate when a formula is evaluated in relation to when the report is run.

To use one of the above functions, insert it as the first line of a formula, followed by a semi colon.

More often than not, the problem of formulas evaluating at the wrong time is in relation to each other, when one formula is reliant on the result from another.

It is easy to lose sight of this in groups of complex formulas, but the effect is clear when viewed in isolation (as the next lesson illustrates).

This problem can be addressed by using the fourth evaluation function:

```
EvaluateAfter(x);
```

This is used as the first line of a formula like the other evaluation functions, where the 'x' is replaced with the formula that must be run before the current one.

NB: Evaluation order has already been covered briefly but this next lesson covers everything in more detail.

Report Name: Evaluation_Order.rpt

Report Requirement: The following lesson shows nothing practical, but does show how to use the EvaluateAfter function and the effect of formula evaluation order.

Report Details:

Table(s)	Fields
Employee	Employee ID

The database fields will not be used at all in this exercise.

1. Create a new formula called "Formula 1" and insert the following code:

    ```
    Global numberVar x;

    x := x + 10;
    ```

2. Save and close the formula.

3. Repeat steps 1 and 2, twice more for formulas; "Formula 2" and "Formula 3".

4. Insert all three formulas into the Detail Section.

5. Preview the report.

The formula all use the same 'x' variable, and all add ten to it. However, the report evaluated them (seemingly) in alphabetical order.

Obviously, having to keep an eye on the alphabetical order of formula names to control their evaluation is tedious enough, but, it doesn't stop there.

Let's assume there was a need for "Formula 2" to increment by ten for each record.

6. Open the formula "Formula 2" and insert the evaluation function of WhilePrintingRecords so it is updated for every row of data returned:

        WhilePrintingRecords;
        Global numberVar x;

        x := x + 10;

7. Save and close the formula and preview the report.

Formula 2 increases by ten every row, as expected. But formula 3, which should be equal to formula 2 plus ten, has dropped from thirty to twenty.

To make formula 3 include the incremented variable in formula 2 the EvaluateAfter function is needed.

8. Open the formula "Formula 3" and insert the evaluation function of EvaluateAfter so it is updated for every row of data returned:

        EvaluateAfter ({@Formula 2});
        Global numberVar x;

        x := x + 10;

9. Save and close the formula and preview the report.

At first glance, this looks correct: formula 3 is the same value as formula 2 plus ten.

However, now formula 2 is incrementing in steps of twenty as it is taking into account the increase made to 'x' in formula 3.

This is a problem when using global variables.

10. Open the formula "Formula 2" and change the 'x' for a 'y':

```
WhilePrintingRecords;
Global numberVar y;

y := y + 10;
```

11. Save and close the formula and preview the report.

Both formulas are now displaying as required.

This exercise has highlighted two main things:

1. Don't use global variations in formulas which will be evaluated at the same time.

2. The order in which formula are evaluated can have an impact on their results, but can be controlled implicitly with the EvaluateAfter function.

Take a few moments to play around with the evaluation time for the three formulas and note how it alters their results. Viewing this in isolation will help your understanding when dealing with more complex formula.

Formulas and Subreports

Subreports are used primarily in one of two situations:

1. Information from a different database needs to be displayed in the same report as the original data but no logic link exists between the two.

2. The same information needs to be displayed by different groupings that would otherwise conflict. A common example of this is a summary section at the top of a detail report.

In either case (more so for the latter) the need to pass values from the main report to the subreport is quite common and makes subreports a lot more useful than without.

Report Name: Subreport.rpt

Report Requirement: The following exercise is going to produce a report that displays both the top 5 Countries, and the top 10 Customers both based on last year's sales. Any customers which are located in one of the top 5 Countries is to be highlighted green.

The main report will display the top 5 Countries, the subreport, the customers.

Report Details:

Table(s)	Fields	Filters	Group(s)
Customer	Country Customer ID Last Year's Sales	Top 5 based on a Sum of Last Year's Sales	Country

Suppress the Detail Section and Group Footer, and empty the Report Footer If you created the report using the Expert.

Create the following subreport and place it in the Report Footer (do not add any Subreport Links).

Subreport Details:

Table(s)	Fields	Filters	Group(s)
Customer	Country Customer ID Customer Name Last Year's Sales	Top 10 based on a Sum of Last Year's Sales	Customer ID

Drag and drop Customer Name and Country fields from the Detail Section to the Group Header.

Suppress the Detail Section and Group Footer, and empty the Report Footer If you created the report using the Expert.

Preview the report.

The two separate sets of information are displayed.

NB: This is the basis of dashboard display and is a hugely popular way of displaying a selection of unrelated data (though usually with charts).

However, the final step requires certain lines in the subreport to be colored based on results in the main report.

We have already looked at Local and Global scope variables in **Variable Scope and Types** Chapter.

To pass data to a subreport requires the use of Shared variable scope.

1. In the main report, create a new formula called "frmCountryList".

2. Add an array declaration with a scope of Shared:

```
Shared stringVar array astrCountries;
```

3. Enter the code to increase the size of the array each time it is called and populate the new space with the Country:

```
Redim Preserve astrCountries[UBound(astrCountries)+1];

astrCountries[UBound(astrCountries)] :=
{Customer.Country};

astrCountries[UBound(astrCountries)];
```

4. Save and close the formula, then insert it into the Group Header Section.

5. In the subreport, open the formula editor for the color option for the Group Header.

6. Declare a Shared array of the same name and type as previously set up for the main report:

```
Shared stringVar array astrCountries;
```

NB: astrCountries will contain the values it was assigned in the main report.

7. Compare the Country field in the subreport with astrCountries, and change the background color of the Group Header Section accordingly:

```
If {Customer.Country} In astrCountries Then
        crGreen
Else
        crWhite;
```

8. Save and close the formula.

9. Preview the main report.

The customers in the subreport are now highlighted in green if they belong to any of the top 5 Countries.

With this ability to move values from the main report to any subreports is a powerful tool which opens up a wide range of possibilities, usually based upon two main methods:

- Single parameters can be used to impact all subreports without the user being asked numerous times for the same choices.

- The results of complex calculations in the main report can be passed to numerous subreports.

NB: Shared variables pass information 'down' to subreports, but information cannot be passed 'up'.

Formulas Manipulating Parameters

Another avenue of manipulation is also made available when applying formulas to subreports, and that is to use parameters to pass values to the subreport (rather than just for linking data).

This subject almost belongs in the third section as a clever hint, but is included here for completeness.

Parameters exist as a means to pass data into a report. Most often, this takes the form of users being prompted to enter criteria to filter a report (and also control formatting, with a little formula knowledge).

But Crystal Reports also uses parameters to pass data and link to subreports.

With a little cheating this can be used to pass a variety of information to subreports with a minimum of work.

This next lesson is going to allow the user to pick one of three font colors for both the main report and the subreport.

The first step is to set up the parameter for the main report.

1. Create a discrete, string based parameter called "prmSelectColor" with the default settings of:

> Black
> Red
> Blue

2. Save and close the parameter.

3. Open the Formula Editor for the Font Color of any field/text box in the report and change it's color based on the parameter:

```
If {?Select_Color} = "Black" Then
        crBlack
Else If {?Select_Color} = "Red" Then
        crRed
Else
        crBlue;
```

4. Save and close the formula and use the Format Painter to apply this change to all the other items in the main report.

To pass the parameter value to the subreport, we could create a Shared variable in the main report as before, and then refer to it in the subreport.

But it is possible to pass the parameter directly to the subreport.

5. Right click on the subreport and select "Change Subreport Links". Link the prmSelectColor parameter to any string field.

6. Open the subreport in design mode and delete the generated code from the Record selection. Save and close the empty formula.

Under the parameter heading in the Field Explorer there is now a parameter called "Pm-?prmSelectColor". This contains the user's choice of color in the main report.

7. Open the Formula Editor for the Font Color of any field/text box in the report and change it's color based on the parameter:

```
If {?Pm-?prmSelectColor} = "Black" Then
        crBlack
Else If {?Pm-?prmSelectColor} = "Red" Then
        crRed
Else
        crBlue;
```

8. Save and close the formula and use the format Painter to apply this change to all the other items in the subreport.

9. Preview the main report.

The subreport font color is changed based on the option selected. Refresh the report a couple of times and try the different color options.

This method of passing values to subreports can also be used to pass formula, and database field values can also be passed in this manner.

It is just a case of setting the required item as a link and then deleting the generated code in the subreport selection criteria.

Conditional Formatting With Formulas

As previously seen, anything within Crystal Reports with the formula Icon next to it can be manipulated using the methods already covered.

The scope for tailoring reports with formula is extensive, in particular, formatting reports based on various conditions (field content and/or user's parameter selections).

Most the exercises so far have resulted in a formula that produced a data type the same as found in a database.

Most formatting options are controlled by a Boolean True or False. Either the formatting is applied or not. But in some cases, the Formula Editor will provide options not usually available.

For example: when controlling the color of text or a section, the Formula Editor will provide a list of default colors as well as an RGB Function to 'mix your own'. Or if controlling a line on a field, the following options are available:

- crSingleLine
- crDoubleLine
- crDashedLine
- crDottedLine
- crNoLine

One of the main advantages of this level of control is that many reports with similar content can be rolled into one.

Report Name: formatting.rpt

Report Requirement: Cover some of the more common formatting available.

Report Details:

Table(s)	Fields
Employee	Last Name
	First Name
	Position

When formatting formulas or database fields, the same changes usually need to be made to numerous objects at once.

There are two ways to do this, which are illustrated now.

1. Create a boolean parameter called "prmDisplayBlueBackground".

2. Select all three of the title database fields via lassoing them, or clicking on each one in turn while holding down the CTRL key.

3. Right click on the selection and pick 'Format Objects…" from the popup menu.

4. Select the Border Tab. Click the formula Icon next to the Background and enter the following code:

```
If {?prmDisplayBlueBackground} = True Then
        Color(50, 10, 255)
Else
        crSilver;
```

5. Save and close the formula, and OK the format Editor Window.

6. Preview the report, selecting True for the parameter.

Obviously, the crBlue could have been used, rather than making a blue via the Color Function. However, most companies have their own distinct colors that require 'mixing' to suit.

7. Preview the report, selecting False for the parameter.

NB: The fields are either blue or silver as would be expected with the If Statement supplied. But when viewed in Design Mode, the Background is clear as the formula is not evaluated until the report is run.

8. Right click on the Last Name Field, and select the Font Tab.

9. Click the formula Icon next to the Background and enter the following code:

```
If {Employee.Position} = "Sales Representative" Then
        crBoldItalic
Else
        crItalic;
```

10. Save and close the formula, and OK the format Editor Window.

11. Preview the report.

The Last Name Field's font is affected by the contents of the Position Field, and is evaluated to either be Italic, or Bold and Italic.

To transfer this formatting to the other fields is simple.

12. Right click on the Last Name Field and select format Painter from the popup menu.

13. Hold down the ALT Key and click on the other two fields. Press the ESCAPE Key when finished.

14. Preview the report.

The formatting is copied to the other fields for the formula, just as it would for any other formatting. Sometimes it is necessary to continually format titles and other objects usually represented via text boxes within a report. However, text boxes do not have the same range of formula controlled attributes.

15. Create a number parameter called "prmSetFontSize".

16. Right click on the Last Name Field, click on the Format Field and select the Font Tab.

17. Click the formula Icon next to the Font and enter the following code:

       {?Set Font Size};

18. Right click on the Last Name Field and select format Painter from the popup menu.

19. Hold down the ALT Key and click on the other two fields.

20. Try and apply the format Painter to the text box fields.

The format Painter cannot apply the font formula to the text boxes.

21. Press ESCAPE and right click on the text box and click on Format Text, and select the Font Tab.

Oddly, there are no formula icons for anything on the Font Tab. However, if you are implicitly controlling the font size of the fields within a report, the chances are, that the titles need to be controlled also.

22. Cancel the format Editor Window and delete the three title text boxes.

23. Create the three following formulas, with their respective text:

Formula Name	Formula Code
frmLastName	"Last Name";
frmFirstName	"First Name";
frmPosition	"Position";

24. Place each formula above its respective field.

25. Right click on the Last Name Field, select the Format Painter and apply it to the three formulas.

26. Preview the report.

Experiment with a few different values for the Font Size by refreshing the report and entering different numbers for the prmSetFontSize parameter.

The formulas used for titles now resize with the fields.

In the case of the Position Field, it does not take much variation before the confines of the field size restrict it.

27. Right click on the Position Field and select "Object Size and Position".

28. Click on the formula Icon next to Width field and enter the following code:

        {?Set Font Size} * 100;

29. Save and close the formula, and OK the Object Size and Position Window.

30. Preview the report.

This quick formula with handle a range of Font Sizes, but is not perfect and treats all the fields the same.

For a more robust solution, see the Chapter **Dynamically Resizing Text to Fit** in Section Three.

Another subject covered in more depth in Section Three, is the value of being able to Suppress Sections based on user input, and in particular being able to switch between a Summary or a Detail style Report.

However, this has various other uses.

In this exercise, the Employee Photo is going to be optional in the report.

1. Insert the Photo Field into the Detail Section.

2. Create a boolean parameter called "prmHidePhoto".

3. Right click on the Photo and select "Format Graphic".

4. Click the formula Icon next to the Suppress, and enter the following code:

        {?prmHidePhoto};

5. Save and close the formula, and OK the format Graphic Window.

6. Preview the report twice, once selecting True to the prmHidePhoto parameter, and then False.

The photo is shown or not, depending on the select made for the parameter. However, even suppressed, the photo leaves a photo sized space in the report which is not ideal.

NB: The formula could have been written in the form of an If Statement:

```
If {?prmHidePhoto} = True Then
        True
Else
        False;
```

This is a perfectly valid, though long winded way of writing the formula.

If the parameter was worded differently as "prmShowPhoto", the user would select True to suppress the photo and the following formula would be needed to reverse it:

```
If {?prmShowPhoto} = True Then
        False
Else
        True;
```

To correct the formatting issue with the suppressed photo, the photo needs to be moved into a separate Section and that Section to be suppressed.

7. Open the Section Expert, highlight 'Details' and click on Insert.

8. Highlight 'Details a' and tick the "Underlay Following Sections".

9. Highlight 'Details b', click on the formula Icon for "Suppress (No Drilldown) and enter the following code:

```
{?prmHidePhoto};
```

10. Save and close the formula.

11. Click OK to close the Section Expert.

12. Drag and drop the photo into Details b Section, resize Details a Section to remove the space left by the photo.

13. Preview the report twice, once selecting True to the prmHidePhoto parameter, and then False.

Now, the eport is correctly formatted whether the photo is shown, or not.

This is also very useful for providing the user with an option to include charts or subreports (or not).

Charts

Nothing in a chart can be controlled via a formula. This can be hugely limiting when developing reports based on user parameters.

Two common requirements regarding charts are to have the option to choose the chart type and/or to select what data to display.

Both of these requirements can be met by using formulas indirectly.

Report Name: Charts.rpt

Report Requirement: Allow user selection of chart type and the data being charted.

Report Details:

Table(s)	Fields	Filters
Orders	Customer ID Employee ID Order ID Payment Received	{Orders.Order Amount} > 9000;

1. Create a string parameter called "prmChartContent", and set two default values:

   > Customer
   > Employee

2. Create a string parameter called "prmChartContent2", and set two default values:

   > Orders
   > Paid

3. Create a formula called "frmCustomerOrEmployee" and enter the following code:

```
If {?prmChartContent} = "Customer" Then
        {Orders.Customer ID}
Else
        {Orders.Employee ID};
```

4. Insert a group based on the frmCustomerOrEmployee.

5. Create a formula called "frmOrdersOrPaid" and enter the following code:

```
If {?prmChartContent2} = "Paid" Then
        Count({Orders.Payment Received}
        ,{@frmCustomerOrEmployee })
Else
        Count({Orders.Order ID},{@
frmCustomerOrEmployee });
```

6. Insert a chart into the Report Header.

7. In the 'On Change of' panel, add the formula frmCustomerOrEmployee.

8. In the 'Show Value(s)' panel add the formula frmOrdersOrPaid.

9. Click OK to save and close the chart.

10. Preview the report.

Four variations of chart content are now possible based on the selections made by the user.

All that remains is to provide equally controllable titles for the chart. Because the titles within a chart cannot be controlled by a formula, formulas must be created to replace them.

11. Right click on the chart, select Chart Options and the Titles Tab.

12. Delete the default titles and click on OK.

13. Create a formula called "frmChartMainTitle" and enter the following code:

```
If {?prmChartContent2} = "Orders" Then
        "Total Of Orders By " & {?prmChartContent}
Else
        "Total Of Paid Orders By " & {?prmChartContent};
```

14. Save and close the formula.

15. Insert the formula frmChartMainTitle above the chart in the position of the original Chart Title, size and reformat to suit.

16. Create a formula called "frmChartDataTitle" and enter the following code:

```
If {?prmChartContent2} = "Orders" Then
        "Total Of Orders"
Else
        "Total Of Paid Orders";
```

17. Save and close the formula.

18. Insert the formula frmChartDataTitle to the left of the chart, size and reformat to suit (including rotating the text 90 degrees if required).

19. Insert the parameter 'prmChartContent' beneath the chart, size and reformat to suit.

20. Preview the report.

Refresh the report a few times with different values. The new formula based titles may need moving around and reformatting to be agreeable with the varying dimensions of the chart.

Controlling the type of chart is a lot less elegant. The only way, currently, to let a user choose between a Bar Chart or Line Chart is create a copy of each chart and suppress the one(s) not selected by the user.

NB: Older versions of Crystal Reports do not enable the copy/paste of charts. If that is the case, skip Step 24 and create another chart by repeating the steps; 6-9.

21. Create a string parameter call "prmBarOrLineChart" with the following defaults:

> Bar Chart
> Line Chart

22. Right click on the chart and select format Chart and on the 'Common Tab' click on the formula Icon next to 'Suppress'. Enter the following code:

```
If {?prmBarOrLineChart} = "Bar Chart" Then
        False
Else
        True;
```

23. Save and close the formula and OK the format Chart Window.

24. Highlight the chart, and press CTRL C to copy it, then CTRL P.

25. Place the new copy of the chart exactly over the original.

26. Change the new chart to display data as a Line Chart.

27. Right click on the new chart and select format Chart and on the 'Common Tab' click on the formula Icon next to 'Suppress'.

28. Enter the following code:

```
If {?prmBarOrLineChart} = "Line Chart" Then
        False
Else
        True;
```

29. Save and close the formula and OK the format Chart Window.

30. Preview the report.

Refresh the report a few times and try different combinations of parameter selections.

The user can now control what data appears in the chart and how the chart displays that data.

NB: When creating a conditional format for a series of overlaid objects, always focus the If Statement on showing the object if selected, rather than suppressing it if it isn't.

This If Statement would work as well as the one in Step 22 to suppress the Bar Chart:

```
If {?prmBarOrLineChart} = "Line Chart" Then
        True
Else
        False;
```

However, if it is decided at a later date to create an Area Chart, that if Statement would need amending to:

```
If {?prmBarOrLineChart} in [ "Line Chart", "Bar Chart"]
Then
        True
Else
        False;
```

And the suppress formula for the Line Chart would also need changing if it had been written in a similar manner.

Cross-Tabs

Like a chart, nothing in a cross-tab can be controlled via a formula.
This can also be limiting when developing reports, but can be resolved
in a manner similar to the method used for the chart.

1. Insert a new Report Header Section beneath the chart to contain
    the cross-tab.

2. Insert a cross-tab into the Report Header b section.

3. Setup the cross-tab with the following values:

Panel	Value
Columns	CustomerOrEmployee
Rows	OrdersOrPaid
Summarized Fields	Max of OrdersOrPaid

4. OK to close the Cross-Tab Expert.

NB: The 'Summarized Fields' does not have the option to not
summarise a field (unlike the charts) and a type of summary has to be
select. By selecting the 'Maximum' (Max) summary operation, only one
value will be displayed as if no summary had been selected.

5. Preview the report.

6. The cross-tab will need resizing and reformatting to fit on one
    page without spilling across and causing the creation of 'side
    pages'. Changing all the number fields to have no decimal
    places will help reduce the cross-tab Width.

7. Refresh the report a few times trying different combinations of
    parameter options.

The cross-tab content and grouping varies in much the same way as
the chart.

Using Document Constants

Several values are available to formulas based on the properties of the report itself. These can be used to handle a variety of situations.

They are accessed under the "Document Properties", "Print State" and "Variable Constants" folders in the Function Window.

The functions in the Document Properties Folder are particularly useful for personalising reports to specific user requirements or the times at which a report is run. The **Drilldown Reports and Formulas** Chapter uses the DrillDownGroupLevel constant from the "Print State" Folder.

At the time of writing it is not possible to directly control the Page Orientation property for a section.

But this can be worked around if necessary, and is a good example of how these functions and constants can be used to control a report based on when it is viewed rather than by the data it contains.

Report Name: PageOrientation.rpt

Report Requirement: Allow user control of the page orientation.

Report Details:

Table(s)	Fields
Product_Type	Product Type ID Product Type Name Description

Additional Setup:

Change the Report Orientation to Landscape.

Insert a second Detail Section and copy all the fields from the original Detail Section so that the two Sections look identical.

Set the Description Field in the Details 2 Section to only expand to a maximum of 2 lines.

Set the Page Orientation for Details Section a, to Portrait.

Extend the Description Field in the Details Section b to the extreme right of the report.

1. Create a boolean parameter called "Show Full Description".

2. Open the Supress property for "Detail Section a" and enter the following code:

    {?Show Full Description};

3. Open the Supress property for "Detail Section b" and enter the following code:

    NOT {?Show Full Description};

4. Preview the report and select "True" when prompted.

The report displays in Landscape with a full length Description field.

5. Refresh the report and select "False" when prompted.

The report displays in Portrait with an edited Description field.

NB: The report creates a new page after every change in orientation. To prevent superfluous pages it is necessary to repeat the above process for every section within the report.

Common Formula Errors and Problems

Some times things go wrong. And unfortunately the available debug tools are sadly lacking in even the most recent versions of Crystal Reports.

The good news is that any problem is usually caused by one of only a few things, many of which have been covered in the tutorials in previous chapters.

The following is a quick checklist with solutions for the most common problems.

Bad Data

This is the number one cause of problems with reports and should be the first thing to be checked.

Bad data can cause a myriad of problems, some of which can be hard to identify, but here are a few examples of what can happen:

1. Date/time fields which are supposed to hold meaning time but have actually default to Midnight can cause date comparisons to error.

    On systems which have manual input as well batch updates from other systems can have both defaulted times and meaningful times in the same field.

    The only way to 'fix' this issue is to amend the report to use only the date segment of the field for any comparisons.

2. Date formatting is another potential problem, as a report may be run on a system with either English or US date formats (the

month and day are reversed) if the report is set to us the System Default Date.

In this case, the date formats need to be implicitly stated in the report, which should be done anyway as a matter of good practice.

3. Databases with "Upper case only" set will not always match on mixed or lower case selection criteria, causes amounts of data to be lost.

    Use the UpperCase Function when filtering against database fields for both the database field and the value which is being compared.

4. Unexpected field content can cause havoc with reported statistics. If the report is producing spurious results investigate what is actually being reported on.

    In many cases it will be an extra job priority no one told you about or an exception to the usual data ("Well, if it's weekend work….").

    The easiest way to identify these exceptions is to create a separate report grouped by the field in question

    NB: Easier still is to run a SQL select Distinct command on the field, but a means to access the database other than through Crystal Reports is not always available.

5. Decimal place values attached to whole numbers can cause problems in the same manner as times on date fields. A number field formatted to hide values after the decimal place will still include them in comparisons or calculations.

    Use the Truncate function to simply drop the values after the decimal place, or the Round function to round the decimal value up/down.

Nulls

Discussed in detail in the **Nulls** Chapter, Nulls can be the cause of numerous problems. A field containing a Null, when used in a comparison will not return True or False, but produces a value of Null.

Variable Scope

If the scope for a variable is not implicitly defined, it will use the default of Global. This means that if a formula uses a variable which has the same name as one used by another formula, both formulas will affect it.

The easiest way to remove this problem is to always implicitly state the variable scope for every variable as Local, unless there is a specific need to share a variable between formulas.

Examples of the impact this can have are covered in the **Correct Formula Order** Chapter.

For Loops

For loops will evaluate as True when they have successfully completed, regardless of what calculations are within the loop or what they evaluate to.

This means that any formula ending with a For Loop will always evaluate as True.

The solution is to ensure that the result from the contents of a For Loop are passed into a variable and that variable is the last thing to be referenced in the formula.

See the **Loops** Chapter for details.

Order of Evaluation

This is related to Variable Scope and is discussed in detail the Chapter **Variable Scope and Types**.

If a variable in one formula shares the same name with a variable in another formula, there is a good chance it will be affected by both unless it is defined with the Scope of Local.

The easiest way to avoid/rectify this problem is to implicitly set the scope for all variables.

Formulas Not Evaluating In Time.

This is a rare problem and very hard to identify (unless you know what to look for), and as such can cause hours of frustration.

When a formula takes too long to evaluate, eventually, Crystal Reports will display the report anyway with whatever value the partially complete formula happens to contain at the time.

This timing issue can be identified by opening the formula in preview mode, amend the formula in some minor way (like a space or comment at the end of the code), saving the changed code will force the formula to rerun. If it displays the correct value(s), refresh the report again.....if the formula produces the desired result now: it is a timing issue.

The solution is to split all the formula processing in two. Run the first half of the formulas in the main report, then pass the results via Shared variables to a subreport that holds the second half of the formulas.

SECTION TWO

Using Formulas for Complex Solutions

How to Use Section Two

The exercises in Section One were deliberately short in order to focus on the individual formula elements.

Some of those exercises have practical applications in report design, but the real strength in formula writing is when all the separate component parts are used together.

To illustrate this point, this entire section is dedicated to the creation of one formula laden report that uses a wide selection of the subjects already covered.

The added bonus of this section is that it creates a very complicated, and oft requested, reporting solution.

Creating a Calendar Report

The basis of this exercise is the development of a calendar style report.

For the month of October in 2009, the following table should be
displayed:

Mon	Tue	Wed	Thur	Fri	Sat	Sun
28	29	30	1	2	3	4
5	6	7	8	9	1	11
12	13	14	15	16	1	18
19	20	21	22	23	24	25
26	27	28	29	30	31	1

Due to the nature of reporting and Crystal Reports in particular,
producing a report in the style of a calendar is particularly tricky.

Displaying a date which the database holds information for is fine, but
what about the dates that have nothing stored against them and do not
exist in the database?

There are several parts to this solution:

- Identify the required month and calculate which days to display.

- Format the report into a calendar style grid

- Identify and format the database data required to display in the report.

- Add the data into the calendar grid.

Identify the required month and calculate which days to display.

Because this report does not need data to be developed, and because it is highly likely to be useful to many readers, the database will not be added until the end of the exercise.

As will soon be obvious, the formulas in this section are very involved. Full listing of the code is available in the Appendix B, and also via download from this website:

www.Scry-Business-Intelligence.com

1. Create a blank report with no database associated with it.

2. Create a date parameter called 'The First Of The Required Month'.

This parameter will be used to calculate which month the report displays.

The report has seven columns, once for each day of the week.

One formula per column will be used, with each day within the month identified within the formula as separate array elements.

First, the formula for Monday is created, which will be eventually copied and amended for the other days.

NB: Single quotes will be used in these formulas to aid the use of HTML for later formatting.

3. Create a formula called 'frmMonday' and add the following code:

```
Local dateVar x :=
(
If DayOfWeek({?The First Of The Required
Month},crMonday) = 1 Then
    {?The First Of The Required Month}
Else If DayOfWeek({?The First Of The Required
Month},crMonday) < 1 Then
    {?The First Of The Required Month} -
DayOfWeek({?The First Of The Required
Month},crTuesday)+7
Else
    {?The First Of The Required Month} -
    DayOfWeek({?The First Of The Required
    Month},crTuesday)
);
```

This code is a little different to how things have been done previously.

The date variable 'x' is populated by the result of the If Statement.

The If Statement takes the selection from the parameter and uses the DayOfWeek function to determine the starting value for the calendar.

Taking the calendar grid example above, the 01/10/2009 is a Thursday, so the formula offsets the value for 'x' to 28/09/2009.

With 'x' set, the formula can now create an array to hold the dates for all the Mondays during the calendar period.

4. Add the following code to the formula:

```
Local dateVar array adteMonday := [x, x+7, x+14, x+21,
x+28, x+35];
```

An array of Monday dates is created based on the initial first Monday stored in x, then incremented by seven for each possible week in the month.

In the case of October 2009, this will produce the following list:

```
28
05
12
19
26
```

To view these values in the report using the HTML functionality as illustrated in the **Formatting Within a Formula** Chapter.

5. Add the following code to the formula:

```
'<b><DIV ALIGN = "CENTER"> ' &
ToText(Day(adteMonday[1]),0,'') & '</DIV></b></br>' &

'<b><DIV ALIGN = "CENTER"> ' &
ToText(Day(adteMonday[2]),0,'') & '</DIV></b></br>' &

'<b><DIV ALIGN = "CENTER"> ' &
ToText(Day(adteMonday[3]),0,'') & '</DIV></b></br>' &

'<b><DIV ALIGN = "CENTER"> ' &
ToText(Day(adteMonday[4]),0,'') & '</DIV></b></br>' &
```

Displaying the first four Mondays is straight forward enough. But fifth and sixth dates may or may not need to be displayed.

This depends on which day of the week the month ends and how many weeks long it is.

The following If Statements evaluate whether or not to display a Monday.

6. Add the following code to the formula:

```
(If adteMonday[5] = DateAdd('M',1,{?The First Of The
Required Month}) Then
   ""
Else If adteMonday[5] > (DateAdd('M',1,{?The First Of
The Required Month})+(7-
DayOfWeek(DateAdd('M',1,{?The First Of The Required
Month}),crMonday))) Then
   ""
Else If adteMonday[5] > DateAdd('M',1,{?The First Of The
Required Month}) - 1 Then
   '<b><DIV ALIGN = "CENTER"> ' &
ToText(Day(adteMonday[5]),0,") & '</DIV></b></br>'
Else
   '<b><DIV ALIGN = "CENTER"> ' &
ToText(Day(adteMonday[5]),0,") & '</DIV></b></br>' ;)&
(
If adteMonday[6] = DateAdd('M',1,{?The First Of The
Required Month}) Then
   ""
Else If adteMonday[6] > (DateAdd('M',1,{?The First Of
The Required Month})+(7-
DayOfWeek(DateAdd('M',1,{?The First Of The Required
Month}),crMonday))) Then
   ""
Else If adteMonday[6] > DateAdd('M',1,{?The First Of The
Required Month}) - 1 Then
   '<b><DIV ALIGN = "CENTER"> ' &
   ToText(Day(adteMonday[6]),0,") & '</DIV></b></br>'
Else
   '<b><DIV ALIGN = "CENTER"> ' &
   ToText(Day(adteMonday[6]),0,") & '</DIV></b></br>');
```

7. Save and close the report.

These two If Statements are constructed with three parts to test for all the end of month possibilities.

The first condition checks to see if the Monday date is the same as the first Monday in the next month. If it is, it means that the entire week is in the next month and should not be displayed.

If that is not the case, the Else If tests to see if the Monday is in the first full week of the next month, again, if it is, it should not be displayed.

The second Else If checks to identify whether the Monday is in a partial week of the next month. If so, the date is displayed.

The final Else assumes that if none of the above criteria have been met, the Monday is within the target month and displays it.

NB: The last two conditions produce the same results at this stage, but will come in useful later.

This formula is not complete yet, but does display the dates for all the Mondays now.

8. Insert the formula in the Report Footer Section.

9. Right click on the formula and select 'Format Field' and change the 'Text Interpretation' to 'HTML Text'.

10. Preview the report.

When prompted select the first of any month. The report should list all the Mondays that are needed in order to display that calendar month.

Rerun the report several times for different months and check the results against a calendar.

Now all that remains is to add the correct data to the correct date and control the length of each day on the calendar to preserve the formatting.

Identify and format the database data required to display in the report

To populate the calendar grid with data, a single formula will be created that populates an array with all the required information split into the correct days within the month.

A couple of extra formulas are going to be used to make it easier to reuse this report with other databases.

First, a formula which will eventually hold the date field from the database is created with a default value:

1.　Create a new formula called 'frmDate' and enter the following code:

    Date(2009, 10, 12);

2.　Save and close the formula.

The default date here is a Monday to allow testing and will be used throughout the report in lieu of a real date field.

The second default formula acts as a placeholder for the data to be displayed in the calendar.

3.　Create a new formula called 'frmInfo' and enter the following code:

    'This is test data for use in the calendar report.';

4.　Save and close the formula.

The text is deliberately long to highlight some formatting issues which arise with reports of this type.

All that is required now is an array to hold these values.

The first step is to create an array with the correct number of elements:

5. Create a new formula called 'frmCalendarSetup' and enter the following code:

```
Global stringVar array astrCalendar;

Redim astrCalendar[Day(DateAdd('M',1,{?The First Of
The Required Month})-1)];

"array Setup";
```

6. Save and close the formula and insert it into the Report Header Section.

The DateAdd function adds one month to the date enter via the parameter field, then one day is subtracted. The result is the last day of the month selected by the user.

This is then used to set the number of elements in the array.

7. Create a new formula called 'frmCalendar' and enter the following code:

```
EvaluateAfter ({@frmCalendarSetup});
Global stringVar array astrCalendar;
```

The next step is to populate the array with the database fields.

8. Add the following code to the formula:

```
If Len(astrCalendar[Day({@frmDate})]) > 1 Then
    astrCalendar[Day({@frmDate})] :=
astrCalendar[Day({@frmDate})] & '</br>' & {@frmInfo}
Else
    astrCalendar[Day({@frmDate})] := {@frmInfo};
```

9. Save and close the formula.

10. Insert the formula into the Detail Section.

11. Preview the report.

The report currently only has one value to show, and that is what is displayed.

This segment of code uses the day of the date field to identify the correct element, and then checks to see whether it is empty.

If it is empty, it inserts the field to be displayed. If not, a return (in HTML) is added before the new value to ensure it starts on the next line.

Now this data just needs building into the calendar grid.

Add the data into the calendar grid.

Because of the work previously done, this is incredibly straight forward. The array needs adding into the 'frmMonday' formula and it's individual elements referenced by the days we already have recorded for Monday.

1. Open the frmMonday formula and insert the following line at the beginning of the code:

   ```
   EvaluateAfter ({@frmCalendar});
   Global stringVar array astrCalendar;
   ```

This ensures that the array has been populated before its contents are used in the calendar.

2. After this line:

   ```
   '<b>' & ToText(Day(adteMonday[1]),0,'') & '</b></br>' &
   ```

   Insert this:

   ```
   (If Day(adteMonday[1]) < 7 Then
   astrCalendar[Day(adteMonday[1])] & '</br>' Else  '</br>')
   &
   ```

The If Statement checks that the first Monday is within the month and displays the data if that is the case.

3. After this line:

   ```
   '<b>' & ToText(Day(adteMonday[2]),0,'') & '</b></br>' &
   ```

   Insert this:

   ```
   astrCalendar[Day(adteMonday[2])]& '</br>' &
   ```

This places the data for the second Monday under that Monday's date. There is no need to check the validity of the second Monday, as it will always be in the correct month.

This method is repeated for the rest of the formula:

4. After this line:

    '<b>' & ToText(Day(adteMonday[3]),0,'') & '</b></br>' &

    Insert this:

    astrCalendar[Day(adteMonday[3])]& '</br>' &

5. After this line:

    '<b>' & ToText(Day(adteMonday[4]),0,'') & '</b></br>' &

    Insert this:

    astrCalendar[Day(adteMonday[4])]& '</br>' &

6. After this line:

    '<b>' & ToText(Day(adteMonday[5]),0,'') & '</b></br>' &

    Insert this:

    astrCalendar[Day(adteMonday[5])]& '</br>' &

7. After this line:

    '<b>' & ToText(Day(adteMonday[6]),0,'') & '</b></br>' &

    Insert this:

    astrCalendar[Day(adteMonday[6])]& '</br>';

8. Save and close the formula.

9. Preview the report for the first of October 2009.

NB: This code can be viewed in it's entirety in Appendix B.

The data from frmInfo is displayed under the correct Monday as identified in frmDate.

To test this further:

10. Open the frmDate formula and amend the code to the following:

    Date(2009, 09, 28);

11. Save and close the formula.

12. Preview the report for the first of October 2009.

The calendar is empty. The date, while displayed in the calendar, is outside of the selected month.

13. Open the frmDate formula and amend the code to the following:

    Date(2009, 10, 19);

14. Save and close the formula.

15. Preview the report for the first of October 2009.

The calendar displays the test data under the fourth Monday, the 19th, as dictated by the frmDate value.

The report now collects the data for a particular month and splits it by day, as well as recording the empty dates in the month.

All that remains now is to format the formula and duplicate it for the other days in the month.

Format the report into a calendar style grid

Now, the depth of each day needs formatting. This is not normally an issue as the depth of an individual field is usually controlled by the section it resides in.

In this case though, frmMonday is one field that can be of unknown height depending on the number of rows returned.

In isolation this is not a problem, but when frmTuesday and the other days are created, it is likely they will all be different lengths and resulting calendar will look confusing and the calendar style grid will be compromised.

Several options exist for controlling the size of each day, all of which fall into two distinct groups:

- Truncate the data displayed to fit in a set size.
- Resize all the boxes to match the biggest returned.

Both have pros and cons. The first option can cause data to not be displayed, whereas the second option can produce huge reports which spoil the accessible calendar format which is the whole point of this report.

As it is always better to have too much data than to have missing data, the second option will be implemented.

There are two factors which control how many rows frmMonday may vary by:

- The length of the data displayed and whether it wraps round to more than one line.
- The number of separate data items held and their associated 'return'.

What is required is a separate formula which identifies the longest element and pads out all the other elements to match.

1. Create a new formula called "frmPadElements" and add the following code:

```
WhilePrintingRecords;
Global stringVar array astrCalendar;

Local numberVar a;
Local numberVar b;

Local numberVar intElementSize;
Local numberVar intPadding;
```

This code creates the variables which will be needed to complete the formula and is set to run after all records are read in to ensure that the array variable astrCalendar is populated.

2. Add the following code:

```
For a := 1 To UBound(astrCalendar) Do
(
        intElementSize := 0;
```

The For Loop will run through each of the array elements in turn.

Firstly thing done is the intElementSize is set to zero.

Now, the formula needs to look at each part of each element and measure how many rows it contains.

3. Add the following code:

```
For b := 1 To UBound(Split(astrCalendar[a], "</br>")) Do
(
        intElementSize :=  intElementSize +
(RoundUp(Len(Split(astrCalendar[a], "</br>")[b])/23));
);
```

The separate parts of each element are delimited by "</br>", so this is used by the Split function to separate it into separate parts.

Each of these parts are then measured using the Len function, and the result is divided by 23 as that is roughly the number of characters per line.

As any partial line still takes up a full line in the report, the RoundUp function is used.

The results for each part of the element are added to the intElementSize.

4. Add the following code:

```
If intElementSize > intPadding Then
        intPadding := intElementSize-1;
);
```

The value in intElementSize is compared to the intPadding formula. If the intElementSize is larger, it is placed in intPadding.

The end result of this is that intPadding will hold the largest number of rows held in the astrCalendar array.

This number is now used to pad out the smaller elements so they are all the same size.

5. Add the following code:

```
For a := 1 To UBound(astrCalendar) Do
(
        intElementSize := 0;

        For b := 1 To UBound(Split(astrCalendar[a],
"</br>")) Do
           (
```

```
        intElementSize :=  intElementSize +
(RoundUp(Len(Split(astrCalendar[a], "</br>")[b])/23));
        );
```

This code is very similar to the first For Loop and just loops through the elements and calculates the number of lines they will generate in the report.

6. Add the following code:

```
If intPadding > intElementSize Then
        astrcalendar[a] :=astrcalendar[a] &
ReplicateString("</br>",((intPadding) - intElementSize)+1)
Else
        astrcalendar[a];
    );
```

Using the difference between intPadding and intElementSize, ReplicateString adds the correct number of 'returns' to pad all elements out to the same size.

And finally…

7. Add the following code:

```
intPadding+1;
```

8. Save and close the formula.

9. Insert the formula in the Report Footer Section.

The formula will now display the maximum size of an element in the calendar grid.

The frmMonday formula now needs to run after frmPadElements rather than frmCalendar.

10. Open frmMonday and change the EvaluateAfter to:

EvaluateAfter ({@frmPadElements});

11. Amend the Else part of the If Statement for the first Monday from:

'</br>'

To:

ReplicateString('</br>', {@frmPadElements})

This change ensures which even a day that does not fall within the month will formatted correctly.

The same issue also needs to be addressed for the days displayed after the month, though this is not as important as it will not affect formatting in any major way.

NB: The following step consists of inserting a couple lines into each If Statement and moving some ampersands. If any problems are encountered, check the code listing in Appendix B or the available download.

12. Change the If Statements for the fifth and sixth Monday to match the code below:

```
(If adteMonday[5] = DateAdd('M',1,{?The First Of The Required
Month}) Then
    ""
Else If adteMonday[5] > (DateAdd('M',1,{?The First Of The
Required Month})+(7-DayOfWeek(DateAdd('M',1,{?The First Of
The Required Month}),crMonday))) Then
    ""
Else If adteMonday[5] > DateAdd('M',1,{?The First Of The
Required Month}) - 1 Then
    '<b><DIV ALIGN = "CENTER"> ' &
    ToText(Day(adteMonday[5]),0,'') & '</DIV></b></br>' &
```

```
      ReplicateString('</br>' , {@frmPadElements})
Else
   '<b><DIV ALIGN = "CENTER"> ' &
   ToText(Day(adteMonday[5]),0,'') & '</DIV></b></br>'&
   astrCalendar[Day(adteMonday[5])]& '</br>' ;) &

(
If adteMonday[6] = DateAdd('M',1,{?The First Of The Required
Month}) Then
   ""
Else If adteMonday[6] > (DateAdd('M',1,{?The First Of The
Required Month})+(7-DayOfWeek(DateAdd('M',1,{?The First Of
The Required Month}),crMonday))) Then
   ""
Else If adteMonday[6] > DateAdd('M',1,{?The First Of The
Required Month}) - 1 Then
   '<b><DIV ALIGN = "CENTER"> ' &
   ToText(Day(adteMonday[6]),0,'') & '</DIV></b></br>' &
   ReplicateString('</br>' , {@frmPadElements})
Else
   '<b><DIV ALIGN = "CENTER"> ' &
   ToText(Day(adteMonday[6]),0,'') & '</DIV></b></br>' &
   astrCalendar[Day(adteMonday[6])]& '</br>';);
```

13. Save and close the formula.

14. Preview the report.

The separate day elements within frmMonday are all displayed with a uniformed size regardless of content.

The final step now is to create the other days of the month based on the frmMonday formula.

15. Copy frmMonday and rename it as "frmTuesday".

16. Find and Replace "adteMonday" for "adteTuesday".

17. Change the "crTuesday" in the Else part of the first If Statement to "crWednesday".

18. Change the first If Statement to compare it to Tuesday (ie 2) rather than Monday (1):

> If DayOfWeek({?The First Of The Required Month},crMonday) = 2 Then

And:

> Else If DayOfWeek({?The First Of The Required Month},crMonday) < 2 Then

19. Add one to the DateAdd in the If Statements for both the fifth and sixth Tuesdays:

> If adteTuesday[5] = DateAdd('M',1,{?The First Of The Required Month})**+1** Then

And:

> If adteTuesday[6] = DateAdd('M',1,{?The First Of The Required Month})**+1** Then

20. Save and close the formula.

21. Repeat steps 17 to 19 for the rest of the week, copying adteTuesday to adteWednesday and so on, until creating adteSunday.

22. A slightly different approach is needed to cope with the last day of the week. Replace the first If Statement with the following:

> If DayOfWeek({?The First Of The Required Month},crMonday) = 7 Then
>   {?The First Of The Required Month}

```
Else If DayOfWeek({?The First Of The Required
Month},crMonday) < 7 Then
    {?The First Of The Required Month} -
    DayOfWeek({?The First Of The Required
    Month},crSunday)+8
Else
    {?The First Of The Required Month} -
    DayOfWeek({?The First Of The Required
    Month},crSunday)+1);
```

Apply the rest of the changes in steps 17 to 19.

23. Format the page as landscape, and insert each of the day
    formulas into the Report Footer Section. Make each formula
    4cm wide (1.57 inches).

24. Format each formula to be treated as HTML, able to grow as
    required and uncheck the "Keep Together" option.

25. Preview the report.

The first thing which may be apparent is that the day which holds the
test text does not align with the other days in the month. If this is the
case, it will be resolved automatically when reading in real database
data.

Now all that remains is to replace the test data with real data.

Adding Data

With the unused sections suppressed, the report should look like this:

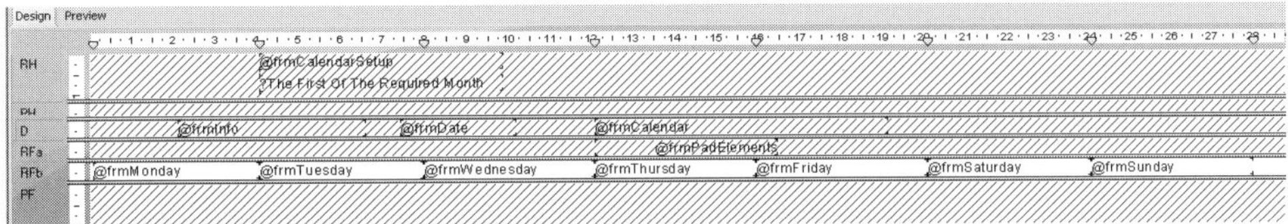

When run for the correct month, it will display the test data, and regardless of month, the correct days will be displayed in the correct order and format.

As with the other exercises in this book, we will use the Xtreme database for illustration purposes. However, the method employed to build this report makes it easy to follow the next steps for any database, so implementing it against your own company database should be straight forward.

The intention of this calendar report is to show which cities have received deliveries to on any days within a selected month.

1. Add the following two tables to the report:

    Customer
    Orders

2. Open the Record selection formula editor and enter the following criteria:

    {@frmDate} In [{?The First Of The Required Month} to dateadd("m",1,{?The First Of The Required Month}) - 1]

3. Save and close the formula.

The way the report works, there is no need to filter the data to control what is displayed, but for the sake of performance, it makes sense not to read in the entire database for the month of data required.

Now, the two formulas created earlier which hold the calendar content and the date need to be populated with database fields.

4. Open the frmInfo formula and replace all the existing code with:

```
If NOT IsNull({Customer.City}) Then
        {Customer.City};
```

5. Save and close the formula.

6. Open the frmDate formula and replace all the existing code with:

```
{Orders.Ship Date};
```

7. Save and close the formula.

This is all that is required to direct the report to real data, whether the Xtreme database or another source, and with a little formatting, looks like this:

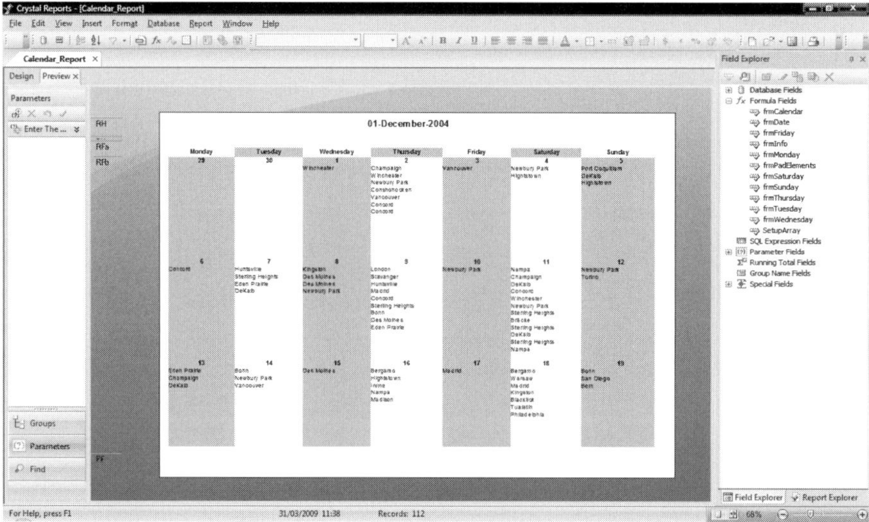

This report would be impossible without formulas and shows what can be achieved by using the separately taught methods in Section One.

Additional Tasks and Tweaks

By many standards this is a complex report, but in some cases, this is just the beginning.

If the calendar is being populated from a database other than Xtreme, some slight tweaks may be required to ensure consistent formatting.

The length of the individual elements may vary, or rather, the space the formula has on the report may vary.

This can be fine tuned by changing the values in frmPadElements, which are currently are set to 23 but may need altering depending on the font used for the content displayed.

Also, because there are no null values in the fields used from the Xtreme Database, no checks have been made. However this may be required if using a different database.

Beyond this, there are functional needs which may be required for the calendar report.

More amendments can be applied to make the calendar report more suitable to specific requirements such as including conditional formatting on the information displayed in the calendar grid via additional code in frmCalendar to highlight customers with a bad credit rating in red.

If a problem arises with duplicate entries in an individual calendar day this can also be accommodated by carrying out checks in frmCalendar before assigning any new value to the array.

SECTION THREE

Useful Formulas

How to Use Section Three

Section Three is a collection of formula written to solve specific problems.

This section can be worked through in a similar manner to Section One, but a lot less detail are provided as to what each part of a formula does, as this has already been covered function by function in Section One.

Working through, or studying, these examples will give the beginner valuable insight into how to build up larger formulas using the basics taught in Section One & Two and may provide solutions to specific requirements.

At the very least, it is recommended the reader familiarise themselves with the solutions presented for future reference.

Every one of the formulas in this section is based on a real life requirement which was resolved in a commercial environment.

ITIL Reporting Period Section

One of the keystones of ITIL service monitoring is the clearance rate of Incidents via the Service Desk and other IT support teams.

These clearance matrices are based on a set time period (usually weekly or monthly) and ensuring all incidents are counted by their correct status during this time frame can be a challenge.

The minimum requirement for meaningful data is usually six fields:

- The Team or Analyst whose performance is being measured.
- Number of Incidents still open from previous periods.
- Number of Incidents opened within the reported period.
- Number of Incidents closed within the reported period.
- Number of Incidents unresolved by the end of the reported period.
- Number of SLA breaches.
- Percent of SLA breaches.

Without formulas, meeting the above requirements would be impossible.

Without using Running Totals, extremely tedious.

The reporting period in this case shall be the last calendar month, but can easily be amended to any date range required.

Looking at each in turn, using invented tables and field names to be as clear and generic as possible:

- **The Team or Analyst whose performance is being measured.**

  This is straightforward enough and should be the Group which contains the incidents owned / handled by the Team or Analyst.

- **Number of Incidents still open from previous periods.**

  This is all incidents which were opened before the reported period and were still open when the period started. This includes incidents closed during the period, after the period end and still not closed when the report was run.

  A Running Total called RT_Open_Before_Period, is used to provide a Distinct Count Summary on the Incident ID. The Running Total Resets on a change of the Team or Analyst Group and Evaluates with the following formula:

```
If {Incident_Table.Open_Date} < minimum(lastfullmonth) Then
        (
        If IsNull({Incident_Table.Closed_Date}) then
                True
        Else If  {Incident_Table.Closed_Date} >=
minimum(lastfullmonth) Then
                True
        Else
                False;
        )
Else
        False;
```

- **Number of Incidents opened within the reported period.**

  Incidents which were opened within the period, regardless of when it was closed, or If not closed at all.

  A Running Total called RT_Opened_In_Period, is used to provide a Distinct Count Summary on the Incident ID. The Running Total Resets on a change of the Team or Analyst Group and Evaluates with the following simple formula:

```
If {Incident_Table.Open_Date} In lastfullmonth Then
        True
```

Else
        False;

- **Number of Incidents closed within the reported period.**

    Any Incident closed during the reported period regardless of when it was opened.

    A Running Total called RT_Closed_In_Period, is used to provide a Distinct Count Summary on the Incident ID. The Running Total Resets on a change of the Team or Analyst Group and Evaluates with the following simple formula:

    If {Incident_Table.Closed_Date} In lastfullmonth Then
            True
    Else
            False;

- **Number of Incidents unresolved by the end of the reported period.**

    Incidents which were created before or during the reported period, which are still open by the end of the reported period.

    A Running Total called RT_Unresolved_In_Period, is used to provide a Distinct Count Summary on the Incident ID. The Running Total Resets on a change of the Team or Analyst Group and Evaluates with the following formula:

    If {Incident_Table.Open_Date} <= maximum(lastfullmonth) Then
            (
        If IsNull({Incident_Table.Closed_Date}) then
                True
        Else If {Incident_Table.Closed_Date} >=
    maximum(lastfullmonth) Then
                True
        Else

```
                False;
         )
   Else
         False;
```

- **Number of SLA breaches.**

  The percent of all the Incidents closed within the period, which breach their SLA.

  A Running Total called RT_SLA_Breach is used to provide a Distinct Count Summary on the Incident ID. The Running Total Resets on a change of the Team or Analyst Group and Evaluates with the following formula:

```
If {Incident_Table.Closed_Date} In lastfullmonth Then
         (
         If {Incident_Table.Closed_Date} >
{Incident_Table.Expected_Date} then
                True
         Else
                False;
         )
   Else
         False;
```

- **Percent of SLA breaches**

  To display the number of breaches as a percent use the RT_Closed_In_Period and RT_SLA_Breach in a formula:

```
(RT_SLA_Breach / RT_Closed_In_Period) * 100;
```

When implemented properly, these formulas will provide the consistent results for previous reporting periods regardless of when the report is run and provide a reliable snap shot of historic data.

An immediate way to test the data validity is that the sum of 'Opened Before Reporting Period' and 'Opened During Reporting Period' should be equal to the sum of 'Closed Within Reporting Period' and 'Open after Reporting Period'.

NB: if the totals do not match up it may be that incidents have been allocated to other Teams or Analysts, so making sure the table structure is correct for what you want to display is paramount. For example; is the Team linked to all incidents or just those they in particular have opened?

This set of formulas can provide a varied set of results due to the manner in which the table structure is linked.

Group Headings (Continued..)

When repeating Group Headings after the first page of a report it is considered good practice to add "continued" to the Group Name.

However, the page numbers are calculated after groups so using the "use a formula as Group Name" is not possible.

Instead:

1. Create the following as a separate formula (NB: there is a space at the beginning of " (Continued)"):

        If pagenumber = 1 Then
                ""
        Else
                " (Continued)";

2. Add a textbox to the Group header.

3. Drag and drop the Group Title into the textbox.

4. Add the formula to the report and format as required.

5. Drag and drop the formula into the textbox after the Group Title.

NB: Remember to check the "Repeat Group Header On Each Page" on the Group Options tab.

This is only suitable when entire reports are based on one group.

Passing Values to Subreports

Values can be passed to subreports via formulas and shared variables. This can be awkward as it requires the variable to be set up in both reports.

A quicker and easier to maintain method is to use subreport links and parameters.

For example, if we wanted to suppress a section on the subreport based on the country specified in the Parent Report.

We could create a formula in the Parent Report with a shared variable and a formula in the subreport of the same type every time we wish to use it.

Or:

1. Right Click on the Subreport and select 'Change Subreport Links…'.

2. use the '>' button to move the 'Country' Field to be linked to the Subreport.

3. Make sure 'Select data in subreport based on field:' is ticked.

4. Click 'OK' regardless of which field is displayed as the linking field in the Subreport.

5. Open the Subreport in edit mode and select 'Selection formulas' on the Report Menu and choose the 'Record…' option.

6. Delete this generated code:

        {Account.Account Number} = {?Pm-Customer.Country}

7. Then save and close the formula (NB: there may also be 'and' above this line that needs to be deleted, and the first field may vary).

So now the Subreport is not linking its data content, but if we expand the Parameters on the Field Explorer 'Pm-Customer.Country' is still there and can be used for display or in any formula.

The method to set this up may seem quite convoluted, but once set up it is much easier to maintain that having to set up shared variables in both the Parent Report and Subreport.

Creating Re-usable Reports

When first embarking upon the development of an extensive reports library, certain steps taken early on can save a vast amount of work later on.

While this is especially true when providing a suite of reports for one organisation, it is also a useful practice which will allow rapid development for different customers as requirements seldom differ in any great way.

So, what is the secret of easily modifiable Reports? Formulas, and lots of them.

The extra few minutes it takes to set up will be paid back time and again, especially when used in conjunction with the Static Cross-Tab in the next section.

The general rules for setting up a report in this way are in three sections.

Section One formula Creation

Begin by creating an empty report. Link to the database, and select a table, but do not add any fields or groups.

Now we need to add the formulas needed to hold the database fields.

Each formula is nothing more than containers for fields. Name them in a distinct and meaningful way.

I suggest the following:

```
_Field01            (Field formula)
_FieldHeader01      (Field Header formula)
_Group01            (Group formula)
_GroupHeader01      (Group Header formula)
```

1. Create separate formulas for each of fields which are likely to be required. Ten is usually the cut off for the amount that can be reasonably displayed.

2. For each of the Field formulas create a Header formula.

3. Create a number of Group formulsa. Again, this is a judgement call and depends on the business, but five is more than enough for most instances.

4. For each of the Group formula create a Group Header formula.

So a standard Report would have _Field01 to _Field10 with matching Header formulas and _Group01 to _Group05 with matching Group Header formulas.

The final list of formulas should look like this:

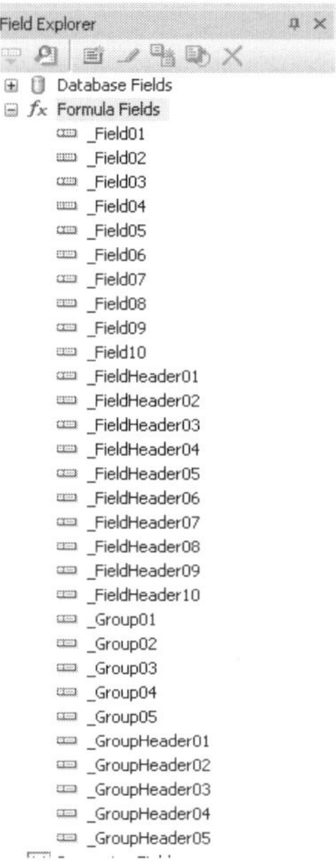

Section Two - Setting Up the Report

This can vary in complexity (as we shall see in the Static Cross-Tab Chapter), but for this first one we'll keep it basic:

1. Add each of the field formulas in order across the Details Section.

2. Add each of the corresponding Header formulas in the Page Header Section.

3. Open each of the five group formulas in turn and insert any database field.

4. Insert three Group(s), one for each of the first three Group formulas.

5. Setup any generic formatting and/or content such as page numbers, company branding, date run etc.

6. Save the Report.

NB: Later you can add the Group Header formulas above each Group Headings and more groups If required.

The report should look like this:

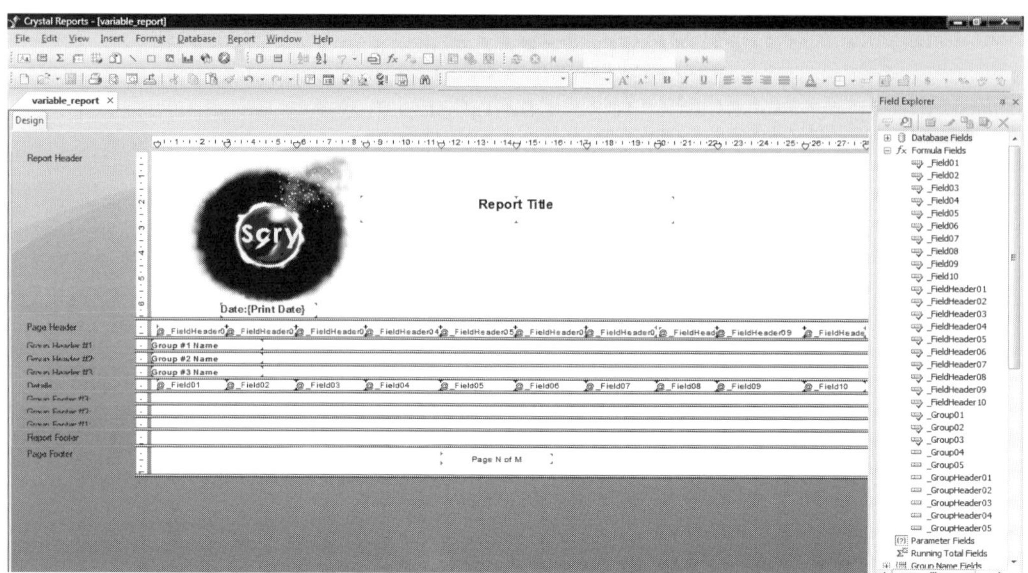

Section Three - Adding Data

To add data to the Report add and link Tables as usual, but instead of adding fields directly to the report, place each field in the field formula which corresponds to where in the Report you want it displayed.

The same with the grouping - add the field you wish to group into the existing group formulas.

NB: Changing the type of field a group is grouping on will cause it to revert to the defaults, so in the case of dates it is worth checking it is grouping in the time span you require.

The only really tedious part of the process is to now type in the column names into each of the Field Header formulas. However, it is usually the case that these must be typed in anyway as database field names are seldom suitable for reports and can the formulas can be reused just as textboxes can.

Once complete, add the required totals and summaries as usual, but base them all on the formulas rather than on database fields.

And that's it. It is quite a bit of extra work for a report which could have been done in half time. But now, if you are required to create a similar report it is just a case of changing the contents of a few of the formulas and all groups and summaries will automatically update too.

Static Cross-Tab Reports

Cross-tabs are a great way of displaying summarised data in a clear and concise manner.

Crystal Reports provides a quick and easy means to insert a cross-tab table into a report via an expert accessible through the Insert Menu.

However, a cross-tab created in this manner is dynamically generated each time the report is refreshed and will only display summaries for data returned.

As always, Crystal Reports cannot report on what is not there. So any summary which returns nothing is not displayed with a '0', but rather, is omitted completely.

This is a problem if the information in the cross-tab is to be compared with a previous report.

The problem is greatly increased if the cross-tab is based on individual groups due to the smaller scope of data available to populate the cross-tab.

This can lead to a series of cross-tabs within one report which are incomparable due the vast differences in the data associated with each group.

Report Requirement: Illustrate the shortcomings of the inbuilt cross-tab Expert.

Report Details:

Table(s)	Fields	Group(s)
Customer	Country	Country
Orders		
Order Details		
Product	Product Color	

1. Insert a group based on the Country field.

2. Place a cross-tab in the Report Header. Use Country for columns and Product Color for rows and summary.

3. Preview the report.

The first thing you will notice is how the width of the cross-tab expands off the page and then across several pages.

This is another problem with dynamic cross-tabs - controlling their formatting.

However, looking down the colors, it appears to be a comprehensive list.

But…

4. Move the cross-tab into the Group Footer.

Now view the report and try to compare color popularity between countries.

The dynamic nature of the cross-tabs, make it difficult or impossible to make direct comparisons.

However, by using formulas it is possible to create a static cross-tab which will display summaries for all columns and rows, regardless of whether or not any data is returned.

NB: This solution uses the same basic steps as outlined in Chapter **Creating Re-usable Reports**.

Only three colors will be used in the following example to illustrate the method.

5. Delete the cross-tab and suppress the Group Header and Detail Section.

6. Move the Group Title field to the Group Footer.

7. Add three text boxes to the Page Header with following contents:

   Black
   White
   Red

8. Create a new Running Total called "rtlBlack" that Distinct Counts, based on the Order ID and resets on the group. Evaluate the Running Total using a formula with this code:

   {Product.Color} = "Black";

9. Insert the Running Total into the Group Footer.

10. Create a new Running Total called "rtlWhite" that Distinct Counts, based on the Order ID and resets on the group. Evaluate the Running Total using a formula with this code:

    {Product.Color} = "White";

11. Insert the Running Total into the Group Footer.

12. Create a new Running Total called "rtlRed" that Distinct Counts, based on the Order ID and resets on the group. Evaluate the Running Total using a formula with this code:

    {Product.Color} = "Red";

13. Insert the Running Total into the Group Footer.

14. Preview the report.

As long as a customer has placed an order at any time, it will appear in the report, even if no products with the required colors have been ordered.

Parameter Based Report Titles

Choosing a meaningful and concise title for a report can be tricky at times, and when a report is based on user selected parameters, the context can change dramatically.

If the parameter is based on a single value, it can just be dragged and dropped into a text box containing the report title and job done. However, if it is a range or multiple values, this method will only display one value and be misleading.

Two separate, handy formulas can be used to build meaningful report titles.

Report Name: Parameter_Titles.rpt

Report Requirement: Display meaningful titles based on user input.

Report Details:

Table(s)	Fields	Group(s)
Customer	Customer ID Customer Name City Country	Order Date (monthly)
Orders	Order Date	

1. Create a ranged date parameter called "prmOrderDate".

2. Create a new formula "frmDateTitle" and enter the following code to display the extremities of the date parameter:

```
"Records From " & minimum({?prmOrderDate}) & " To " &
maximum({?prmOrderDate}) & ".";
```

3. Save and close the formula and insert it into the Report Header.

This will take the start date input by the user and the end date and build it into a sentence much like:

"Records From 01/03/2010 To 23/04/2010."

Showing multiple user selected parameter values, while similar in concept to displaying a range, the fact that a user may choose one or more values makes the formula more complicated:

4. Create a multiple value string parameter called "prmSelectCountry" with a default list based on the customer country field.

5. Create a formula called "frmTitle" and enter the following code:

```
local stringVar strReportTitle := "Summary Sales Report
for ";
local numberVar intCounter;


If UBound({?prmSelectCountry}) = 1 Then
(
        strReportTitle := strReportTitle &
{?prmSelectCountry}[1];
)
Else
(
        For intCounter := 1 to
        UBound({?prmSelectCountry}) Do
        (
                If intCounter =
                UBound({?prmSelectCountry}) Then
                (
                        strReportTitle := strReportTitle[1 to
                        (Len(strReportTitle)-2)] & " And " &
                        {?prmSelectCountry}[intCounter];

        )
```

```
                Else
                (
                        strReportTitle := strReportTitle &
                        {?prmSelectCountry}[intCounter] & ",
                        ";
                );

        );

    strReportTitle;

);
```

6. Save and close the formula and insert it into the Report Header.

This formula starts the title with "Summary Sales Report for "and adds a comma delimited list of the user's selected parameter values, with an "And" separating the last two items in the list. If only one value has been selected, that single selected parameter is displayed.

There is also a variation on the above formula If you are using the parameter 'Optional' choice to accommodate the 'All' option:

```
For intCounter := 1 to UBound({?prmSelectCountry}) Do
(
        If intCounter = UBound({?prmSelectCountry})
    Then
        (
                strReportTitle := strReportTitle[1 To
                (Len(strReportTitle)-2)] & " And " &
                {?prmSelectCountry}[intCounter];
        )
        Else
        (
                strReportTitle := strReportTitle &
                {?prmSelectCountry}[intCounter] & ", ";
        );
);
```

```
        strReportTitle;


    );
```

There is an added If Statement, at the beginning of the formula. This identifies whether a user who has picked a single value has selected 'All', or a particular discrete value.

If the user has selected 'All', the Report Title will read:

"Summary Sales Report for All Countries"

NB: For more recent versions of Crystal Reports, optional parameters can be used to replace the " All" solution. Personally I prefer the to let the user select "All" when they want all the records, leaving the parameter blank to receive all the records seems counterintuitive.

But for completeness, here is the equivalent optional parameter code:

```
local stringVar strReportTitle := "Summary Sales Report
for ";
local numberVar intCounter;

If HasValue({?prmSelectCountry}) = True Then
(
        If UBound({?prmSelectCountry}) = 1 Then
        (
                strReportTitle := strReportTitle &
                {?prmSelectCountry}[1];
        )
        Else
        (
                For intCounter := 1 to
                UBound({?prmSelectCountry}) Do
                (
                        If intCounter =
                        UBound({?prmSelectCountry}) Then
```

```
                              (
                                      strReportTitle :=
                                      strReportTitle[1 to
                                      (Len(strReportTitle)-2)] & "
                                      And " &
                                      {?prmSelectCountry}[intCount
                                      er];
                              )
                              Else
                              (
                                      strReportTitle := strReportTitle
                                      &
                                      {?prmSelectCountry}[intCount
                                      er] & ", ";
                              );

                      );

              strReportTitle;

          );
  )
  Else
  (
     strReportTitle := strReportTitle & "All Countries
  Included"
  );
```

Warning Messages

On occasion, there is a requirement to provide a report which furnishes the user with a selection of parameter options which if used incorrectly will supply misleading results, or some times nothing at all.

While some (though not all) eventualities can be handled within formulas to limit potential damage in regard to returned data, there will always be some instances which have to be allowed to enable interactive reports to actually be useful.

A good practice, and convenient way, of drawing the user's attention to their incorrect use of the report is to display an error message on the front page.

How obstructive the message is to the use of the report should come down to how erroneous the impact of the contained data is, and is a judgement call.

A discrete message at the top of the first page as a warning about content may be fine for a small transgression, or take up the entire first page so it can just be easily discarded.

However, taking up half the first page with large, red, words of warning will leave no doubt as to the quality of the report's content.

Looking at **Parameter Based Report Titles** Chapter as an example, being able to choose "All" and get all the records returning is a handy tool. However, what if someone chooses "All" and then three other additional values?

This may not sound likely, but if the user is rerunning the report, it is easy to forget to remove the previous parameter values.

So what happens?

If "All" is the first value in the parameter, the report will return everything and ignore any subsequent values. Depending on the style / type of the report, this could prove very misleading.

If "All" isn't the first value, it is treated as one of the discrete values and will be compared directly to the database field. This will not retrieve any data itself, nor will it affect the data returned by the actual discrete values. But if the user was expecting to see "All" the records, the data returned will be a lot less than expected.

Knowing this, we can create an error message to warn anyone reading the Report that its contents may be misleading:

1. Insert an additional section in the Report Header.

2. Create a formula against this section's 'Suppress' property:

```
If UBound({?prmSelectCountry}) > 1 Then
(

        If "All" In {?prmSelectCountry} then
        (
                False
        )
        Else
        (
                True
        );

)
Else
(
        True
        );
```

3. Save and close the formula.

This will suppress the section if the parameter is being used as intended.

4. Now create a formula called "Error_Message" to contain the warning message:

```
If UBound({?prmSelectCountry}) > 1 Then
(
        If "All" In {?prmSelectCountry} then
        (
                If {?prmSelectCountry}[1] = "All" then
                (
                        "All Countries Are Currently Being
                        Displayed Due To The Inclusion Of
                        The parameter Option 'All'.";
                )
                Else
                (
                        "'All' Has Been selected Amongst A
                        Series Of Options for Country,
                        However, Only Named Countries Will
                        Be Displayed.";
                );
        )
        Else
        (
                "No one will ever see this text."
        );
)
Else
(
        "No one will ever see this text."
);
```

This formula will provide one of two messages depending on the manner in which the user has misused the parameter.

5. Place this formula in the new Header Section and format it to be as large and gaudy as you deem fit to get the message across.

6. Additionally, if the want the report to start on the page after the warning message, use this formula against the Header Section's 'New Page After' property:

```
If UBound({?prmSelectCountry}) > 1 Then
(
        If "All" In {?prmSelectCountry} then
        (
                True
        )
        Else
        (
                False
        );
)
Else
(
        False
);
```

There are a myriad of uses for error messages like this, many that will be specific to your organisation. They take a little extra work, but can save a lot of hassle further down the line.

Alternating Section Colors

This is covered at a basic level in the first section of this book. However, this simplistic approach will be unsuccessful on more complication reports and extra work is needed to provide a more robust solution.

Report Name: Formatting.rpt

Report Requirement: Create a more robust means of displaying alternating section colors.

Report Details:

Table(s)	Fields
Customer	Customer ID
	Customer Name
	City
	Country

1. Enter the following formula to alternate Section color for the Detail Section (via the Color Tab on the Section Expert):

> If Remainder(RecordNumber, 2) = 0 Then
> crRed
> Else
> crWhite;

2. Save and close the formula and preview the report.

Every second row is colored red.

NB: It is similar for a Group Section:

> If Remainder(GroupNumber, 2) = 0 Then
> crBlue
> Else

        crWhite;

Both of these methods work as expected, until you conditionally hide a Section or nest Group Sections.

For example, if a report on customers had all customer names with contained the word "Bike" suppressed.

3. Enter the following formula code to the Detail Section suppression option:

```
If {Customer.Customer Name} LIKE "*Bike*" Then
        True
Else
        False;
```

4. Save and close the formula and preview the report.

The formatting is ruined as the suppressed rows are still counted by the row number upon which the coloring formula is based.

By using a running total to manually count the groups or records a more reliable formula to control the section color can be created.

For a conditionally suppressed Detail Section, rather than rely on the record number, create a running total which limits its count summary with the same conditions used to suppress the Detail Section.

NB: The results from the conditions must be reversed.

5. Create a distinct count running total called 'rtRowCount', that the Customer Name field and add an Evaluation formula to limit it to only count the records which are not suppressed:

```
If {Customer.Customer Name} LIKE "*Bike*" Then
        False
Else
        True;
```

6. Amend the Color Tab formula on the Section Expert to use the running total:

```
If Remainder({#rtRowCount},2) = 0 Then
        crRed
Else
        crBlue;
```

7. Save and close the formula and preview the report.

The report now keeps the formatting across all the rows, even if they are suppressed.

Additionally, if you want each new group to start with the same color, set the running total to reset on that group.

Nested groups are a similar problem with a similar solution.

Nested groups will always mess up a color scheme based on the Group Number value, as it counts every individual group regardless of which level of group it is.   This can be resolved using the same method used for Detail Section.

Correct Averages

This is not really formulas related per se, however, I feel it is worth mentioning as a separate issue due to the large number of times I've seen this mistake:

Do not average other averages!

I think that it is because Crystal Reports is based heavily on groups that this error arises so often.

Here is an example of how this happens and how much it can skew results:

Imagine you are providing the average sales for two items in the same week:

> Item A
>
> Pack size 1 = 100 units
> Pack size 2 = 50 units
> Pack size 3 = 50 units
> Pack size 4 = 100 units
> Pack size 5 = 75 units
>
> Average = 75 units

So far, so good. Crystal Reports can group weekly on a date field, and the above could easily be produced within a report.

Now, looking at Item B for the same week:

> Item B
>
> Pack size 1 = 20 units
> Pack size 2 = 20 units

Average = 20 units

So what is the average for both Item A and B?

(75 + 20) / 2 = 47.5

No, it is not.

It's the 7 days total travel divided by 7:

(100 + 50 + 50 + 100 + 75 + 20 + 20) / 7 = 59.3

A big difference in this case because I've deliberately skewed the data to illustrate the point. But in commercial reports this sort of error can be much less obvious and easily go undetected.

Summarising Fields into a List

It is quite common, especially in summary reports, for there to be only one field of interest in the Detail Section. Using the Detail Section to display a single field as a column greatly increases the report's length and hampers readability.

Summarising the contents in a single field as one string field in the Group Footer saves space on the report and gives the user all the information they need at a glance.

Due to the varying nature of report requirements I'm going to provide three solutions, one of which should fit most scenarios.

The simplest just displays all the values as a comma delimited list. This is ideal if each of the single field's contents are unique. If not, duplicates will be listed. The first basic formula is then extended to cater to other scenerios.

Report Name: SummaryList.rpt

Report Requirement: Display all the Order ID's per customer on one line.

Report Details:

Table(s)	Fields	Group(s)
Customer	Customer ID Customer Name City Country	Customer ID
Orders		

Additional Setup:

Move all the fields into the Group Footer and suppress the Detail and Group Header Sections.

At first glance this request sounds straight forward enough, but the trick is to make sure the list resets for every group and any Nulls are catered for.

1. Create a formula called "frmOrderIDs" and enter the following code:

```
Global stringVar strList;
Global stringVar strShowList;
Global numberVar intCounter;

If intCounter = 0 then
        intCounter := 1
Else
        intCounter;

If IsNull({Orders.Order ID}) then
(
        intCounter := intCounter + 1;
        strShowList;
)
Else
(
        If intCounter <= Count({Customer.Customer ID},
        {Customer.Customer ID}) then
        (
                intCounter := intCounter + 1;
                strlist := strlist & ToText({Orders.Order
                ID},0,"") & ", ";
        )
        Else If intCounter = Count({Customer.Customer
        ID}, {Customer.Customer ID}) + 1 then
        (
                strShowList := strlist;
                intCounter := 1;
                strlist := "";
        );
```

```
);

If Len(strShowList) > 0 then
(
        strReverse(Mid(strReverse(strShowList),3));
)
Else
(
        "";
);
```

2. Save and close the formula.

3. Insert the formula into both the Detail Section and the Group Footer Section.

4. Reformat the formula to 'Can Grow' and preview the report.

The Order IDs are listed for each customer without taking up excessive report space.

NB: If this was the only field being displayed, multiple columns could be used instead.

However, if there is a chance of duplicate results in the single field and there is a requirement not to repeatedly display them, then a more intricate solution is needed.

For this, an array could be used to compare each field value to the contents of the array and only add it if not already present. But this can be avoided by simply adding an additional If Statement to the formula above to check if the single field value is already present in the list.

To show the how the next formula works, the Ship Via field shall be listed as it holds duplicates and can be empty.

5. Before creating the formula, insert a Group base on the 'Ship Via' Field and add the following Summary:

Distinct Count on the 'Ship Via', Grouped on the Customer ID

6. Create a formula called "frmShipViaList" and add the following code:

```
Global stringVar strBuilder;
Global stringVar strShowBuilder;
Global numberVar intCounter;

If intCounter = DistinctCount ({Orders.Ship Via},
{Customer.Customer ID}) then
(
        strShowBuilder := strBuilder ;
        strBuilder := "";
        intCounter := 0;
)
Else
(
        strBuilder := strBuilder & GroupName
        ({Orders.Ship Via}) & ", ";
        intCounter := intCounter + 1;
);

strreverse(Mid(strReverse(strShowBuilder),3));
```

7. Save and close the formula and add it to both the Ship Via Group Footer and the Customer ID Group(s) Footer.

8. Reformat the formula in the Customer ID Group Footer to 'Can Grow'.

9. Preview the report.

Each shipping company used by a particular customer is show only once per customer.

The third solution caters to the situations where there is a need to list the single field values and count the number of occurrences too.

This will be achieved by modifying the above formula further.

Before creating the new formula, add the following summary:

Count on the 'Ship Via' Field Grouped on the 'Ship Via' Group.

10. Remove all the other formula from the report.

11. Create a formula called "frmShipViaCount" and add the following code:

```
Global stringVar strBuilder;
Global stringVar strShowBuilder;
Global numberVar intCounter;

If intCounter = DistinctCount ({Orders.Ship Via},
{Customer.Customer ID}) then
(
        strShowBuilder := strBuilder ;
        strBuilder := "";
        intCounter:= 0;
)
Else
(
        strBuilder := strBuilder & GroupName
        ({Orders.Ship Via}) & "(" & ToText(Count
        ({Orders.Ship Via}, {Orders.Ship Via}),0,"") & "), ";
        intCounter := intCounter  + 1;
);

strReverse(Mid(strReverse(strShowBuilder),3));
```

12. Save and close the formula and add it to both the Ship Via Group Footer and the Customer ID Group(s) Footer.

13. Reformat the formula in the Customer ID Group Footer to 'Can Grow'.

14. Preview the report.

The shipping companies used are now uniquely listed with the number of times each customer has used them in brackets to the right.

The results achieved by using the above three methods are usually realised by using subreports, but the above methods are more efficient solutions (subreports require their own, seperate connection to a database). By limiting the use of subreports it becomes viable to use the report itself as subreport.

User Field Selection

For all Crystal Report's strengths, user control is not one of them. If a user requires several similar reports but with some different fields: then numerous reports must be developed.

It is possible to use a parameter and formulas to enable a lot more user control.

Report Name: FieldSelection.rpt

Report Requirement: Allow user control of which fields to include in a report.

Report Details:

Table(s)	Fields
Customer	Customer ID
	Customer Name
	Contact Title
	Contact Name
	Phone
	E-mail
Credit	
Orders	

Additional Setup:

Reach agreement with the user as to the sets of fields they want the option of displaying. In this case, the choice is customer details, order details or credit details.

For each set of fields, insert an additional section into the report section which is going to contain the fields.

In this case, split the Detail Section on this report into three sections.

Copy the Customer ID and Customer Name field into the two new Detail Sections.

Split the Page Header into the same number as the Detail Section, three in this instance.

Copy the Field Headings for the Customer fields into the two new Page Sections.

Place the following fields from the Order Table in Detail B Section:

>Order ID
>Order Amount
>Ship Via
>Shipped

Create the matching Header Fields in Page Header B Section.

Place the following fields from the Credit Table in Detail C Section:

>Credit Authorization Number
>Customer Credit ID
>Amount

Create matching Header Fields in Page Header C Section.

The report should look something like the following:

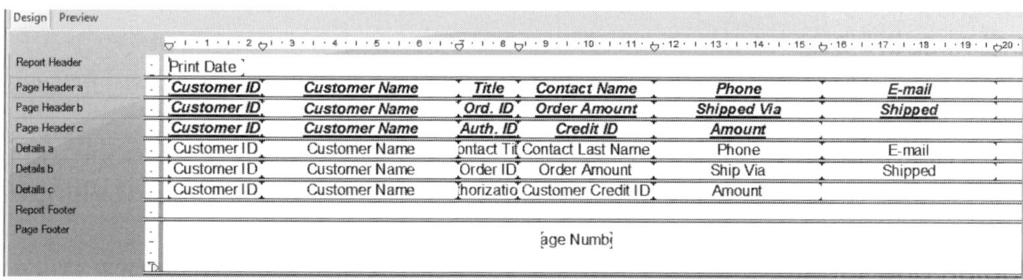

1. Create a string parameter called "prmSelectFields" with three discrete options:

    Customer Details
    Order Details
    Credit Details

2. Create a formula called "frmShowCustomer", which will be used
    to take the user option and display the customer details if
    selected:

    ```
    If {?prmSelectFields} = "Customer Details" then
            False
    Else
            True;
    ```

3. Create a formula called "frmShowOrders", which will display the
    Order details if selected:

    ```
    If {?prmSelectFields} = "Order Details" then
            False
    Else
            True;
    ```

4. Create a formula called "frmShowCredit", to display the Credit
    details if selected:

    ```
    If {?prmSelectFields} = "Credit Details" then
            False
    Else
            True;
    ```

5. Add the frmShowCustomer formula to the suppression formulas
    for Page Header a and Details a.

6. Add the frmShowOrders formula to the suppression formulas for
    Page Header b and Details b.

7. Add the frmShowCredit formula to the suppression formulas for
    Page Header c and Details c.

8.   Preview the report.

The report will display duplicate records due to the nature of the table logic, but with a few refreshes selecting different parameter values will illustrate the method.

The same method can be used to display a different Report Header or different charts.

User Group Selection

This is another way of allowing users control over their reports and to cut down on the volume of reports needed to meet the requirements of the business.

This is very similar in concept to 'Enabling users to select Which Fields to Include' and when used together they can provide a large amount of variation within one report.

Report Name: GroupSelection.rpt

Report Requirement: Allow user control of a report's grouping.

Report Details:

Table(s)	Fields
Customer	Customer ID Customer Name City Country

Additional Setup:

Reach agreement with the user as to the fields they want the option to group the report on. In this case we are going to use 'City', 'Region' and 'Country'.

1. Create a parameter called "prmSelectGroup". Provide the user with three, discrete, options; 'City', 'Region' and 'Country'.

2. Create a formula called "frmGroup" and enter the following code:

```
Select {?prmSelectGroup}
Case "City":
        {Customer.City}
```

```
Case "Region":
        {Customer.Region}
Case "Country":
        {Customer.Country};
```

3. Insert a group into the report based on the frmGroup formula.

4. Insert a Distinct Count Summary based on the Customer ID and grouped by frmGroup.

Now refresh the report and select a group option from the parameter. Both the group changes and the summary field based on this group.

However, there is a problem in that the field chosen to group by is still in the Detail Section. This is not always the case, and may not be a problem when it is, but for the sake of neatness we shall make the potential group fields dynamic.

5. Remove the fields 'City', 'Region' and 'Country' from the Report.

6. Create four formula fields; "frmField01" and "frmField02", "frmHeader01" and "frmHeader02".

7. The intention is to display whichever two of the three haven't been picked for the group. In frmField01 enter the following formula:

```
Select {?prmSelectGroup}
Case "City":
        {Customer.Region}
Case "Region":
        {Customer.Country}
Case "Country":
        {Customer.City};
```

8. And the same again for frmField02, but with the values moved around by one place:

```
Select {?prmSelectGroup}
Case "City":
        {Customer.Country}
Case "Region":
        {Customer.City}
Case "Country":
        {Customer.Region};
```

9. A similar formula is used in frmHeader01 for the Field Header:

```
Select {?prmSelectGroup}
Case "City":
        "Region"
Case "Region":
        "Country"
Case "Country":
        "City";
```

10. And the same again for frmHeader02, but with the values moved around by one place:

```
Select {?prmSelectGroup}
Case "City":
        "Country"
Case "Region":
        "City"
Case "Country":
        "Region";
```

11. Add frmField01 and frmField02 to the Detail Section and the frmHeader01 and frmHeader02 to the Page Header Section.

Refreshing the report and selecting a different parameter option will cause the group to change and the two fields not chosen to appear in the Detail Section.

Formatting Within a Formula

The formatting options available through Crystal Reports allow a wide variety of changes to the appearance of a formula's content.

However, these options must be applied to the formula as a whole. If there is a requirement to format part of a formula things become complicated.

Consider the following sentence as the result of a formula:

> "This *Sales Rep* is the **top seller** in this region."

To recreate the same formatting as above, the sentence would have to be split into five separate formulas, formatted individually, then placed into a textbox:

> "This "
> *"Sales Rep "*
> "is the "
> **"top seller "**
> "in this region."

Fortunately another option is available via HTML tags. So in this example the text would be formatted like so:

> "This <i>Sales Rep</i> is the <b>top seller</b> in this region."

Once the formula is added to the report, go to the Format Editor and the Paragraph Tab.

Change the 'Text Interpretation' via the dropdown box to "HTML Text".

NB: Selecting this option means that any text returned by the formula is treated as HTML. THE FORMULA ITSELF IS INTERPRETED AS CRYSTAL SYNTAX so any calculations within the formula will still be evaluated.

Obviously this option opens a wide variety of possibilities and HTML is a subject in its own right and beyond the scope of this book.

However, here are examples of some of the more common formatting tags:

Font Type:

<span style='font-family:Times New Roman'>   </span>

Font Size:

<span style='font-size:20.0pt'>   </span>

Color:

<span style='color:red'>   </span>

Underline:

<u>   </u>

Bold:

<b> </b>

Italics:

<i>   </i>

New Line:

<p> </p>

NB: Tags can be nested to apply multiple changes to the same text. for example, to apply both 'Bold' and 'Italics' to the same text:

"<b><i>This will have both tags applied.</i></b>"

HTML tags can also be combined with formula variables like any other text.

The following example, when placed in the Detail Section, will increase font size by 2 points for every record:

```
"<span style='font-size:" & ToText(recordnumber * 2,0,"") &
".0pt'> Font is now "& ToText(recordnumber * 2,0,"") & "</span>"
```

Formula Controlled Chart Content

Charts are a great candidate for user interaction, and a lot of users are used to quickly changing chart types and content in Excel.

However, Crystal Reports does not provide any interaction between the user and the chart and no chart properties are controlled by formulas.

In order to provide any sort of user interaction, either the chart as a whole and / or the data it is looking at must be manipulated.

This can be achieved one of two ways:

> 1. Allow different chart types to be selected by the user

> 2. Base the chart content on user defined fields

These two solutions are realised in quite different ways, but of course, they can be combined to provide a wide variety of options.

Allow different Chart types to be selected by the user

This is the more basic of the two solutions, but provides the user with a selection of choices in one report which would otherwise require a variety of reports to display.

Report Details:

Table(s)	Fields	Group
Customer	Customer ID Customer Name	Customer ID
Invoice		

1. Create a bar chart in the Group Footer with the following values:

- On change of: Customer ID
- Show value(s): Sum of Gross Amount

• Set up Axis Labels and Titles to suit

2. Version differences:

    a. If using versions after Crystal Reports 10 Copy and Paste the chart three additional copies in the Group Footer.

    b. If using an earlier version of Crystal Reports you may not be able to Copy and Paste a chart, so have to recreate three additional copies by hand with the changes described in the next step.

3. Change the copied charts (or create them) to be the same as the original except for the following settings:

    1st Copy: change the Chart Type to Line.

    2nd Copy: change Show value(s): Count of 'Invoice #'

    3rd Copy: change the Chart Type to Line and Show value(s): Count of 'Invoice #'

    Change the Chart Titles as required.

4. Create a string parameter called "prmSelectChartType". Provide the user with four discrete options:

    "Invoice Amount Bar Chart",
    "Invoice Amount Line Chart",
    "Number Of Orders Bar Chart"
    "Number Of Orders Line Chart".

5. Add the following code to each of the respective chart's Suppress formula:

    Original:

```
If {? prmSelectChartType } = "Invoice Amount Bar Chart"
Then
        False
Else
        True;
```

1st Copy:

```
If {? prmSelectChartType } = "Invoice Amount Line Chart"
Then
        False
Else
        True;
```

2nd Copy:

```
If {? prmSelectChartType } = "Number Of Orders Bar
Chart" Then
        False
Else
        True;
```

3rd Copy:

```
If {? prmSelectChartType } = "Number Of Orders Line
Chart" Then
        False
Else
        True;
```

When the report is run, the user has the choice of four different charts to choose from via a parameter.

Base the chart content on user defined fields

The second solution is to allow the user to select which fields a chart will be based on.

This is much more versatile, but some restrictions exist due to the limited control available and certain default settings for charts.

How a chart is grouped cannot be altered viable formulas, nor can the type of summary operation used to produce the chart.

But even with these limitations, a wide variety of options is possible.

Report Name: DefinedCharts.rpt

Report Details:

Table(s)	Fields	Group	Filter
Customer Invoice	Customer ID Customer Name	Customer ID	"f" in {Customer.Customer Name};

Additional Setup:

Move Customer Name and Customer ID into the Group Header.

1. Create a string parameter field called "prmGroupedBy" with discrete options of:

> Customer
> City
> Region
> Country

2. Create a string parameter field called "prmSummaryData" with discrete options of:

> Invoices
> Orders
> Sales Reps

3. Create a formula called "frmChangeOfField" and enter the
    following code:

```
Select {?prmGroupedBy}
Case "Customer":
        {Customer.Customer Name}
Case "City":
        {Customer.City}
Case "Region":
        {Customer.Region}
Case "Country":
        {Customer.Country};
```

4. Create a formula called "frmSummaryField" and enter the
    following code:

```
Select {?prmSummaryData}
Case "Invoices":
        {Invoice.Invoice #}
Case "Orders":
        ToText({Orders.Order ID},0,"")
Case "Sales Reps":
        ToText({Orders.Employee ID},0,"");
```

5. Create a bar chart in the Report Header with the following
    values:

    - On change of: frmChangeOfField
    - Show value(s): Count of frmSummaryField
    - Remove Axis Labels and Chart Title (and Sub Title if
      there is one)

6. Split the Report Header Section twice so there is a separate
    section above and below the chart.

7. Add a text box to the 'Report Header Section a' with the
    following text and inserting the parameters where indicated:

"Graph for Total {?prmSummaryData} By {?prmGroupedBy}"

8. In the section beneath the chart insert the prmGroupedBy parameter centred under the chart.

9. In the same section as the chart and to the left, add the prmSummaryData parameter. Format it so the text is rotated 90 degrees. Resize to suit.

NB: Depending on how predictable the X axis data will be, but changing the Axis Label to 45 degrees can greatly increases the chances of the chart formatting correctly.

When run, the report can provide a chart based on a variety of data options, selected by the user, with group, summary and report titles which change to match the user's choices.

Before releasing the report to the user, check that all (or at least most) of the possible charts display in a pleasing manner.

It is possible to combine both of these solutions to provide the widest range of possibilities for the user.

NB: avoid producing a report with too many parameters which will become tedious to use.

Counting Working Days Between Two Dates

The DateDiff Function is a quick and easy way to count the days between two dates.

But to only count working days takes a little more work.

Report Name: WorkingDays.rpt

Report Requirement: Create a report which measures the days elapsed between a delivery being ordered, and it shipping.

Report Details:

Table(s)	Fields	Filters
Orders	Ship Date Order Date	WeekDay({Orders.Order Date}) In 2 To 6 And WeekDay({Orders.Ship Date}) In 2 To 6;

The filter is to limit the dates shown to week days as this would be the case for a company which only operates on weekdays and would require this formula.

NB: Two to six is Monday to Friday in the DayOfWeek Function.

1. Create a formula called "frmWorkingDaysElapsed" and enter the following code:

```
numberVar intCount;
numberVar intdays := 0;

If IsNull({Orders.Ship Date}) Then
(
        0;
```

```
)
Else
(
        For intCount := 1 To DateDiff( "d",{Orders.Order
Date},{Orders.Ship Date}) Do
        (
                If DayOfWeek(DateAdd( "D",intCount,
                {Orders.Order Date})) In 2 To 6 Then
                        intdays := intdays +1;
        );
);

        intdays;
```

2. Save and close the formula and insert it into the Detail Section.

3. Preview the report.

The formula will count the working days between the order being received to when the items are physically dispatched.

NB: Removing the filter will not cause the formula to fail, but any orders received or shipped on a weekend will produce partial, and in this case, misleading results.

Dynamic Hyperlinks and Emails

As already covered, formulas can be used to concatenate text. If this is combined with the Crystal Reports Hyperlink format option, reports can create dynamic links to websites, documents or email address.

Report Name: HyperlinksEmails.rpt

Report Requirement: Create a clickable URL based on the employee name.

Report Details:

Tables	Fields
Employee	Employee ID
	First Name
	Last Name
	Initial

The formula to build an email address is straight forward assuming it is made from the Last Name and the Initial from the First Name.

1. Create a formula called "frmEmaiLink" and enter the following code:

   {Employee.Last Name} & {Employee.First Name}[1] & "@xtreme.com";

2. Save and close the formula and add it to the Details Section of the report.

3. Right click on the formula field and select the format Field and open the Hyperlink Tab.

4. Check the 'An E-mail Address' option.

5. In the 'Hyperlink information' section, click the formula icon and enter:

> {@frmEmailLink};

6. Save and close the formula.

NB: It is possible to type the original formula directly into Hyperlink formula, but has been placed in a separate formula so it can be referenced elsewhere if required.

It may also be the case that a web address is held within a database, which does not even have to be displayed within the report, but can be used to apply a URL to a company logo or name.

In the above example, frmEmaiLink can be assigned to the Employee ID field.

7. Right click on the Employee ID field and select the format Field and open the Hyperlink Tab, then check the 'An E-mail Address' option.

8. In the 'Hyperlink information' section, click the formula icon and enter:

> {@frmEmailLink};

9. Save and close the formula.

The original formula field can now be removed from the report if required, as the user can now just click on the Employee ID for the email link.

Creating Fuzzy Links to Subreports

Linking a subreport to a parent report is usually a straight forward process but in certain cases there is not a perfect match between fields, especially when reporting on two or more different data sources.

Where a logical link exists in some form, a formula can be created to amend the fields until they match.

Report Name: FuzzyLinks.rpt

Report Requirement: List all the customers for the USA, then a subreport to show the other customers nearby. 'Nearby' in this case means that the first two digits of the postal code match.

Parent Report Details:

Tables	Fields	Filters
Customer	City Customer Name Postal Code	{Customer.Country} = "USA";

1. Create a formula called "frmPostalCodeLink" with the following code:

   {Customer.Postal Code}[1 To 2];

2. Group by the Postal Code Field and move all the fields into the Group Header and suppress the Detail Section.

Subreport Details:

Tables	Fields	Filters
Customer	City Customer Name Postal Code	{Customer.Country} = "USA";

3. On the Links Tab add the frmPostalCodeLink and select the Postal Code from the Subreport drop down.

4. Add a second link, Postal Code for the Parent Report and the same again for the subreport.

5. The Filter Formula for the subreport will be automatically populated with the link criteria:

```
{Customer.Country} = "USA"
And
{Customer.Postal Code} = {?Pm-@frmPostalCodeLink}
And
{Customer.Postal Code} = {?Pm-Customer.Postal Code}
```

6. This needs amending to the following:

```
{Customer.Country} = "USA"
And
{Customer.Postal Code} [1 to 2] = {?Pm-
@frmPostalCodeLink}
And
{Customer.Postal Code} <> {?Pm-Customer.Postal Code}
```

7. Save and close the formula (NB: The last line of the formula is to stop a customer listing itself as nearby).

8. Refresh the report.

Each customer in the Parent Report will have a list of customers who are nearby.

This is a simple example to illustrate the theory, but many more complex formulas can be created and used in this manner.

A common problem arises when an ID field in one database is being held as a string, while also being held as a number in the original database.

Dynamically Resizing Text to Fit

There is often a requirement to display text of varying lengths within a finite amount of space. The field can be set to a certain number of rows, but any text beyond that will not be displayed.

By resizing the font size depending on the length of the text the amount of truncated text can me minimised.

Report Name: ResizingText.rpt

Report Requirement: Dynamically set the font size based on the length of a field's contents.

Additional Setup:

If using a version of Crystal Reports previous to version 10, then before creating this report:

Open the Employee table in Access and change the Employee Notes field data type from Memo to Text with a length of 500.

Report Details:

Table(s)	Fields
Employee	Notes

1. Open the Formula Editor for the Notes field's font size and enter the following code:

```
If Len({Employee.Notes}) > 25 Then
        8
Else If Len({Employee.Notes}) > 15 Then
        10
Else
        12;
```

2. Save and close the formula.

3. Refresh the report.

The font size will vary depending on the number of characters within the Notes field.

Controlling Graphical Content

In the rare event that images are stored on the database, Crystal Reports can load and display them as with any other embedded graphic.

The difficulty arises when embedded graphics need to be dynamically amended depending on the report's content.

This can occur for a variety of reasons:

- Company logo variations between departments.
- Different maps for report driven locations.
- Loading previously generated charts exported as graphics.
- Product illustrations.
- Any graphic relating to data stored on the database that is held separately.

Report Name: GraphicalControl.rpt

Report Requirement: List the details of all employees, but only display the photo for sales representatives.

Report Details:

Table(s)	Fields
Employee	Employee ID Last Name First Name Position

1. Go to the Insert Menu and select "Insert Picture".

2. Navigate to the Xtreme Employee photo graphics. These are usually located in the same directory as the database.

3. Select any one of the images and insert it into the Detail Section to the right of the fields already added.

4. Right click on the Graphic and select "Format Graphic…", then click on the Picture Tab.

5. Open the formula associated with "Graphic Location" and enter the following formula (NB: the path for the variable strDirectory may need amending to reflect your installation):

```
stringVar strDirectory := "C:\Program Files\Microsoft
Office\Office10\Samples\";


If {Employees.Title} = "Sales Representative" Then
        strDirectory & {Employees.Photo}
Else
        "";
```

NB: The blank string in the second half of the If Statement will not cause an error, nor will pointing to an invalid directory or nonexistent graphic.

6. Save and close the formula.

If the report was refreshed now, any member of staff not a Sales Representative would display the Graphic initially inserted.

7. Click on the Common Tab, open the formula associated the suppress option and enter the following formula:

```
If {Employees.Title} = "Sales Representative" Then
        False
Else
        True;
```

8. Save and close the formula and refresh the report.

Graphics are only displayed for Sales Representatives, other employee's photographs are left blank.

NB: This example is very simplistic, but is extremely useful when combined with string manipulation which can be used to dynamically build different directories or file names based on database records or user selected values via parameters.

Elapsed Time in Minutes and Seconds

The function DateDiff is very effective at finding the difference between two Date or DateTime fields as a specific unit, ie; Hours, Months, Seconds.

To display the difference between two dates as two units, like minutes and seconds, or hours and minutes, some additional work is required.

Report Name: ElapsedTime.rpt

Report Requirement: Calculate the time elapsed between an order being received to it being shipped.

Report Details:

Table(s)	Fields
Orders	Order Date Shipped Date

1. Create a formula called "frmElapsedWeeks" and enter the following code:

```
stringVar intLowestOutput;

numberVar intBiggerUnit;
numberVar intLowestUnit;

numberVar intDiffElapsed := DateDiff("D",{Orders.Order Date}, {Orders.Ship Date});

intBiggerUnit := truncate(intDiffElapsed / 7);

intLowestUnit := remainder(intDiffElapsed,7);

intLowestOutput := ToText(intLowestUnit,0,"");
```

```
            If Len(intLowestOutput) = 1 then
                    intLowestOutput := "0" & intLowestOutput;

            ToText(intBiggerUnit,0,"") &":" & intLowestOutput;
```

2. Save and close the formula and insert it into Detail Section.

3. Preview the report.

The formula displays the number of weeks between the two dates.

The basic rule is to find the total number of the lowest unit required and use that to calculate the larger unit. So the above formula can easily be amended by changing the interval type in the DateDiff Function and changing the Remainder and Division lines to suit.

Minutes & Seconds

```
    intBiggerUnit := Truncate(intDiffElapsed / 60);

    intLowestUnit := Remainder(intDiffElapsed, 60);
```

Hours & Minutes

```
    intBiggerUnit := Truncate(intDiffElapsed / 60);

    intLowestUnit := Remainder(intDiffElapsed, 60);
```

Days & Hours

```
    intBiggerUnit := Truncate(intDiffElapsed / 24);

    intLowestUnit := Remainder(intDiffElapsed, 24);
```

Weeks & Days

```
    intBiggerUnit := Truncate(intDiffElapsed / 7);
```

```
intLowestUnit := Remainder(intDiffElapsed,7);
```

Months & Weeks

```
intBiggerUnit := Truncate(intDiffElapsed / 4);
```

```
intLowestUnit := Remainder(intDiffElapsed,4);
```

It is also possible to extend the formula to allow the elapsed time to be displayed by three units, in this case it is: Week, Days and Hours (NB: the hours part of the total will always be zero as the database stores all times as 12 am).

4. Create a new formula called "frmElapsedAll" and enter the following code:

```
stringVar intLowestOutput;
stringVar intBiggerOutput;

numberVar intBiggestUnit;
numberVar intBiggerUnit;
numberVar intLowestUnit;

numberVar intDiffElapsed := DateDiff("H",{Orders.Order
Date}, {Orders.Ship Date});

intBiggestUnit := truncate(intDiffElapsed / 168);

intBiggerUnit := remainder(truncate(intDiffElapsed /
24),7);

intBiggerOutput := ToText(intBiggerUnit, 0,"");

If Len(intBiggerOutput) = 1 then
        intBiggerOutput:= "0" & intBiggerOutput;

intLowestUnit := remainder(intDiffElapsed, 24);
```

```
intLowestOutput := ToText(intLowestUnit,0,"");

If Len(intLowestOutput) = 1 then
        intLowestOutput := "0" & intLowestOutput;

ToText(intBiggestUnit,0,"") & ":" & intBiggerOutput & ":" &
intLowestOutput;
```

5. Save and close the formula and insert it into the Detail Section.

The time elapsed is displayed in Weeks, Days and Hours.

NB: It may seem logical to use the Time or DateTime Variable types to display the output from a formula like this. However, if the total numbers are greater than expected (example: there is more than 24 hours) these variables will error when the report is refreshed (even though the Formula Editor will allow you to save without a warning).

Controlling Object Size and Position

While objects are usually placed, sized and positioned manually in a report, it is possible to 'fine tune' their dimensions via the Object Size and Position window (available through the 'right click' menu on most objects or the format Menu).

The addition of formula Icons to the X co-ordinate and width makes it possible to dynamically control an object when a report is run.

Two quirks exist with how formula values are treated:

1. Numbers in the Object Size and Position window are displayed in inches or centimetres (depending on configuration). The formula manipulates these values using a mix of inches/centimetres And Twips.

2. The number supplied by the formula DOES NOT replace the values already displayed in the Object Size and Position window.

The first quirk is easy enough to accommodate with the knowledge that a Twip is 1/1440 of an inch and about 1/567 of a centimetre.

If creating a report which is likely to be amended by others, it could be a worthwhile investment to begin each formula with the following code:

```
numberVar intInchTwip := 0;
numberVar intCentTwip := 0;

numberVar intInchRatio := 1440;  //comment out this line
numberVar intCentRatio := 567;  //or this one depending
on system settings

numberVar intTwip;

If intInchTwip <> 0 then
```

```
        intTwip := intInchTwip * intInchRatio
Else
        intTwip := intCentTwip * intCentRatio;

    intTwip;
```

Then, comment out either intInchTwip or intCentTwip to the required number and use intTwip in whatever additional calculations are needed to obtain the desired results.

The best way to get used to the second quirk is to play about with the values and view the target object in both Preview and Design to observe the what effect the changes have.

In particular, note what happens to the object when it is resized in Preview Mode and then view it in the Design View.

Report Requirement: Dynamically move the Description field to the left if the user selects to hide the Name field.

Report Details:

Table(s)	Fields
Product_Type	Product Type ID Name Description

1. Create a boolean parameter called "PrmHideProductName".

2. Conditionally suppress the Name Field and it's title based on the parameter option with the simple code:

   ```
   {?PrmHideProductName};
   ```

3. Right click on Name field and select 'Size and Position…'. Make a note of the X value, and whether CM or Inches are being used. On my report it is CM and an X value of 6.180.

4. Right click on Description field and select 'Size and Position…', make a note of this X value (10.890 on my report) and open the Formula Editor for the X value.

5. Enter the following code, substituting my numbers for your equivalents (replace the 567 for 1440 If inches are required):

```
If {?PrmHideProductName} Then
    -((10.890 - 6.180)* 567);
```

6. Save and close the formula.

7. Repeat the same code for the title textbox for the Description Field and enter the same code for the X value.

8. Preview the report.

Choose 'True' when prompted by the parameter.

The Name Field is hidden and the Description Field is moved to the left to take its place.

This formula behaves very differently to the usual way. Taking the above numbers as an example, this formula should return: -2670.57. Even allowing for Crystal Reports translating the number into CM (or Inches), -4.71 would still be returned and the field would be placed off the page to the left.

What actually happens is that Crystal Reports applies the result to the value in the X value after translating it to Twips. So in this case, 4.71 is subtracted from 10.890.

If this was not confusing enough, amend the X Value formula to the following:

```
If {?PrmHideProductName} = true Then
    10.890 - ((10.890 - 6.180)* 567);
```

Based on what we have already seen, this should return 6.180, which should be automatically added to 10.89 to set the X value to 15.60.

Preview the report. Obviously, this is not the case and the report is still setting the X Value to 6.180.

Both versions work in the same way despite producing very different numbers and both may be encountered when amending other developer's reports.

Handling Time Differences Under a Second

At the time of writing Crystal Reports does not handle milliseconds either as a field type or (as a direct result of this) within any formula functions. This is not likely to change as most databases do not cater to milliseconds.

Therefore, any field containing milliseconds (or smaller) must be passed to the report via a number or string field.

Report Name: UnderASecond.rpt

Report Requirement: Handle and manipulate milliseconds.

Report Details:

Table(s)	Fields
Orders	Order ID
	Order Date
	Expected Date

Additional Setup:

This example solution requires two text fields to be added to the Xtreme Database's Order table to accommodate the millisecond values:

```
millisecs_start
millisecs_end
```

Once created, add various values between 0 to 99, for test purposes. For ease of testing, it is also advised to change at least some of the two date fields to differences of an hour or less.

NB: Despite holding a number, these fields are added as strings as this is the most common way milliseconds are recorded in order to store the leading zero for single digits.

The object of the following formula is find the time elapsed between Order Date and Expected Date while factoring in the millisecond fields.

1. Create a formula called "frmMilliSecDiff". This is in three distinct sections, part one finds the difference between the dates (which are stored as minutes and seconds) and the milliseconds:

    ```
    stringVar strOutput;

    numberVar intDiffSecs := DateDiff("s", {Orders.Order
    Date}, {Orders.Required Date});

    numberVar intMinutes;
    numberVar intSeconds;
    numberVar intMilli;

    intMinutes := Truncate (intDiffSecs / 60);

    intSeconds := Truncate(Remainder(intDiffSecs, 60));

    intMilli := ToNumber({Orders.millisecs_end})-
    toNumber({Orders.millisecs_start});
    ```

2. The second step to amend the millisecond value, seconds and minutes, if required due to a negative difference between the milliseconds:

    ```
    If intMilli < 0 Then
    (
            intMilli := intMilli + 100;
            intSeconds := intSeconds - 1;
    );

    If intSeconds < 0 Then
    (
            intSeconds := 59;
            intMinutes := intMinutes - 1;
    ```

```
);
```

3. The third, and final, section builds the results into an acceptable format, padding out any single digits with additional zeros:

```
strOutput := ToText (intSeconds,0,"");

If Len(strOutput) = 1 Then
        strOutput := "0" & strOutput;

If Len(ToText (intMilli,0,"")) = 1 Then
        strOutput := strOutput & " 0" & ToText (intMilli,0,"")
Else
        strOutput := strOutput & " " & ToText (intMilli,0,"");

ToText(intMinutes,0,"") & ":" & strOutput;
```

The above formula will display the elapsed time is the below format:

```
Minute Minute : Second Second Millisecond Millisecond
```

For example:

```
23:59 89
```

Any impact on seconds or minutes that the difference between milliseconds may have is taken into account.

NB: The minutes can be more than two digits depending on amount, and this amount can be huge in this report due to the nature of the test data.

To display the date/time with the millisecond field, either drag and drop both fields into a textbox, which allows the date/time to be reformatted, or concatenate them in a formula:

```
{Purchases.Order Date} & " :" & {Purchases.millisecs_start};
```

Currency Converter

When dealing with international reports and different currency types it is easy for a report to be very misleading.

Currency symbols are set within the report and have no relation to which type of currency is used on the database.

The safest way to ensure that a report clearly illustrates the correct currency type is to have the user select currency type via a parameter and amend the report to suit.

Report Name: CurrencyConverter.rpt

Report Requirement: Allow dynamically set currency conversion.

Report Details:

Table(s)	Fields	Group(s)
Orders	Order Amount	Order Date

1. Create a parameter called "prmSelectCurrency" and add the following discrete options:

    Pounds Sterling
    US Dollars
    Euros

2. Create a formula called "frmConverter" and add the following variables:

    numberVar intPounds := 2.06;
    numberVar intEuros := 1.23;
    numberVar intUSDollars := 1;

NB: The Xtreme Database holds currency as US Dollars, so does not need to be converted.

3. Conditionally increase the value of the order amount based on the selection:

```
If {?prmSelectCurrency } = "Pounds Sterling" Then
        {Orders.Order Amount} * intPounds
Else If {?prmSelectCurrency } = "US Dollars" Then
        {Orders.Order Amount} * intUSDollars
Else
        {Orders.Order Amount} * intEuros;
```

4. Save and close the formula and refresh the report.

After refreshing the report with the different parameter options it becomes obvious that while the currency amount is being manipulated, the currency symbol is remaining the same.

5. Right click on the frmConverter and select "Format Field". Click on the Customise Button and select the Currency Symbol Tab.

6. Open the Formula Editor for associated with the Currency Symbol and enter the following code:

```
If {?prmSelectCurrency } = "Pounds Sterling" Then
        "£"
Else If {?prmSelectCurrency } = "US Dollars" Then
        "$"
Else
        "€";
```

7. Save and close the formula and refresh the report.

Now the report will display currency symbols that match the currency type selected by the user.

Steps 4 and 5 will be needed for any additional field relating to currency. For example, if a summary was added based on frmConverter, the summary would need the same formatting applied.

NB: It is also advisable to include the chosen currency within the Report Header for additional clarity.

The above solution is fine when dealing with only one field. When dealing with a number of currency conversions future maintenance should be a consideration.

In particular, the actual conversion rates are currently coded into the formula frmConverter:

```
numberVar intPounds := 2.06;
numberVar intEuros := 1.23;
numberVar intUSDollars := 1;
```

Ideally, these variables should be update dynamically from a database field.

Alternatively, the report can be altered slightly to allow the user input the conversion value themselves.

1. Create a new parameter called "prmConversionValue" with a data type of number.

2. Open the formula frmConverter and replace all the code with the following:

```
{Orders.Order Amount} * {?prmConversionValue};
```

3. Save and close the formula, and refresh the report.

The user will now be prompted to enter a value for the conversion and the prmSelectCurrency parameter does nothing more than select the type of currency symbol to display.

NB: These types of options in a report are very prone to user error and can damage the validity of the report content. In this case, more than before, it is recommended that the choices in the parameter fields are displayed at the top of the report.

Creating a Paired List Report

A straight forward request which can be surprisingly awkward to develop is the need for a report that allows the users to filter on numerous pairs of criteria.

In this example case, the user wants to pick multiple customers within certain countries who are limited by a different amount spent last year for each country.

At first glance this appears simple enough: two multi value parameters, one for countries and one for minimum amount spent.

However, when it comes to writing the Record Selection Formula, there is a problem:

> {Customer.Country} In {?Country}
> And
> {Customer.Last Year's Sales} > {?Minimum Amount};

This filter will return any country selected if it's "Last Year's Sales" is greater than any of the values in the Minimum Amount Parameter.

In order to resolve this issue, each pair of filter values must be compared together.

Report Name: PairedList.rpt

Report Requirement: Allow user control of the page orientation.

Report Details:

Table	Fields
Customer	Customer Name Last Year's Sales Country Postal Code

1. Create a multi-value string parameter called "prmCountryList".

2. Create a multi-value currency parameter called "prmMinimumAmount".

3. Open the Record Selection Formula Editor and enter the following code:

```
numberVar x;
booleanVar blnResult := False;

For x := 1 To UBound({?prmCountryList}) Do
(
        If ({Customer.Country} = {?prmCountryList}[X])
        And ({Customer.Last Year's Sales} >
        {?prmMinimumAmount}[X]) Then
        (
                blnResult := True;
                x := UBound({?Country List});
        );
);

blnResult;
```

4. Refresh the report.

When prompted, enter the various pairs of parameters and experiment with different values.

The report will only display Customers that match both parameters criteria.

An error will arise in the report if there is a mismatch and more of one parameter is entered than another.

Unfortunately there is no way to guarantee a matching pair of parameters, but by wrapping up the code in an If Statement the System Error can be avoided:

5. Open the Record Selection Formula Editor and enter the following code:

```
numberVar x;
booleanVar blnResult:= False;
Global stringVar strErrorMsg := "";

If UBound({?prmCountryList}) =
UBound({?prmMinimumAmount}) Then
(
   For x := 1 To UBound({?prmCountryList}) Do
   (
        If ({Customer.Country} = {?prmCountryList}[X])
        And ({Customer.Last Year's Sales} >
        {?prmMinimumAmount}[X]) Then
        (
                blnResult := True;
                x := UBound({?Country List});
        );
   );

   blnResult;
)
Else
(
        strErrorMsg := "Equal Number Of Parameters Must
        Be Entered";
        blnResult:= False;
);

blnResult;
```

6. Create a formula called "frmErrorMsg", and enter the following code:

Global stringVar strErrorMsg;

strErrorMsg;

7. Save the formula and place it in the Report Header. Format it to have a large font and color red.

8.   Refresh the report. When prompted, enter the parameters from Step 5.

The report does not error, returns no data, but instead displays a message telling the user they have used the report incorrectly.

Error Handling

Some provisions can be made to guide user input, but there is huge scope for contradictory parameter values to be entered or values that will give a false representation of the stored data.

At the time of writing, it is not possible to associate a formula with a parameter to validate user input, therefore the report will run regardless of the parameter values provided (unless the values are bizarre enough to cause Crystal Reports itself to fail!).

But formula can be used to provide the user with a warning message that the contents of a report may be spurious due to their parameter entries.

In some cases, it is suitable to restrict the user by returning a report devoid of data. But it is important to tell the user why no information has been returned, otherwise they may assume it is because there is no suitable data to be displayed.

Rather than base this on a real report, several examples will be provided here.

This is the ideal code structure for a formula to evaluate parameter input:

```
Global stringVar strErrorMsg;

//As many separate If Statements required to cover the most
// likely/harmful user choices.

strErrorMsg;
```

The following, are a list of some common errors:

- Entering a future date. This is not always a bad thing, but can lead to misleading data, especially when averages over time are being used.

- Entering a start date which is after the end date in a date ranged search.

- Entering values in two or more parameters which are so contradictory in nature that no data will ever match.

- Required to enter a certain number of values in a multi value parameter, in this example: 5 different regions need to be added to produce an average of sales for that set sample size.

- Conditional formatting of user input. If a user is expected enter a value of a certain length or type based on an option chosen in another parameter.

There are many more potential errors than these few examples, but hopefully they have provided a guide to the frame work for creating report specific error handling.

The code needed to identify these possible errors is no different to that used for other tasks.

Taking the first example of a future date being used in a date range parameter, a simple If Statement is required:

```
If Maximum({?Date Range}) > Today Then
        strErrorMsg := "Date Range Must Not Be In The
        Future.";
```

Numerous If Statements can be listed, one after the other within the formula to meet a variety of requirements.

Place the completed formula in a prominent position in the Report Header, formatted with a large bold font, colored red.

The second half of the solution for error handling is to force the report to return no data at all to guarantee that the user is not misled (or inadvertently misleads others) by incorrect results.

Then, using the same If Statement conditions as the error handling formula, make the whole record selection dependant on the If Statement being False.

So if the original code was:

```
{database.Shipped_Date} In {?Parameter_Start_Date} To
{?Parameter_End_Date};
```

But there is a concern about users entering future Dates:

```
If {?Parameter_End_Date} < Today Then
        {database.Shipped_Date} In
        {?Parameter_Start_Date} To
        {?Parameter_End_Date};
Else
        False;
```

A practical example of this type of checking can be seen in the Chapter **Warning Messages**. But note how setting the error message and limiting the record selection are done in the same place (ie: the Record selection formula) and the secondary error formula does nothing, except display the result.

This is another equally valid method and it is down to personal preference which is used.

Conditional Page Headers

A common problem with reports is that column headings which repeat on each page are not always required on the last one (or more) pages.

For example: when a Chart / Cross Tab / Summary is placed at the end of a report which does not require the titles used for the fields used for the main data.

To illustrate this, create the following report:

Table	Fields	Filter
Customer	Customer Name Last Year's Sales City Country Postal Code	Country = "USA"

1. Create a chart in the Report Footer with:

    'On Change Of' = Customer Name
    'Show Value' = Last Years Sales

2. Click the 'New Page Before' option for the Report Footer.

3. Refresh the report.

The chart is displayed on a new page which has the Field Titles in the Page Header despite there being no fields beneath them.

For recent versions of Crystal Reports, use the following steps to identify the final page and suppress the Page Header:

4. Open the Section Expert, highlight the Page Header and select the Formula Editor for the 'Suppress' option.

5. Enter the following formula code:

PageNumber = TotalPageCount;

6. Save the formula and refresh the report.

The final page, which contains the chart, does not display the unwanted Field Titles.

NB: For two or more final pages, the formula can be offset, so to affect the last three pages the suppression code is:

PageNumber = TotalPageCount - 2;

For older versions of Crystal Reports, more work is required:

7. Count the number of Detail rows on a page.

8. Open the Section Expert, highlight the Page Header and select the Formula Editor for the Suppress option.

9. Enter the following code, replacing '60' with the number from Step 4:

```
If PageNumber = 1 Then
        False
Else If PageNumber > ((Count({Customer.Customer
Name})/60)+1) Then
        True
Else
        False;
```

10. Save the formula and refresh the report.

The last page of the report displays the chart, but the Page Header is now suppressed (thus removing the Field Headings from view).

11. Change the Record Selection formula to:

{Customer.Country} = "England";

12. Save the formula and refresh the report.

Only three pages are displayed, and the Page Header on the final page is still suppressed.

13. Split the Report Footer into two separate sections.

14. Copy and Paste the chart into the new Report Footer Section.

15. Click the 'New Page After' option for 'Report Footer a' in the Section Expert.

16. Refresh the report.

The last two pages now have a chart on them, but as the Page Header suppression is triggered by the end of the data listed in the Detail Section.

NB: When implementing this solution for real, it is worth running reports of varying length to ensure that the row count per page is accurate, as slight errors can build up over numerous pages and some fine tuning may be required.

Partial DateTime Filters

Filtering a report by DateTime is the same as any other comparison within Crystal Reports.

However, a problem can arise when the user wishes to add parameters a report based on a value which does not contain the same level of detail. So if the user has a DateTime which ends in minutes, and wants to filter the report based on a DateTime field, there is a problem.

If the user's DateTime value is:

> 01/01/2009 09:15

The second value could be padded out:

> 01/01/2009 09:15:00

But this would not match on a comparison with a DateTime of:

> 01/01/2009 09:15:36

And changing the comparison to a 'Greater Than' could contain too much data.

There are some additional issues:

- The user wanting to include seconds when running the report at a later date.

- The user requiring a search that doesn't include minutes either.

The following excerise works through these issues and provides a solution:

Report Name: PartialTimeMatch.rpt

Report Details:

Table	Fields
Order	Customer ID Employee ID Ship Date

NB: To fully see the benefit of this formula, you may need to manually update the Field 'Ship Date' to include specific time values.

1. Preview the report and make a note of a "Ship Date" that contains several records.

2. Create a DateTime parameter called 'Required Date Time'.

3. Open the Report Selection Formula Editor and enter the following formula:

```
If Second({?Required Date Time}) = 0 Then
(
    If Minute({?Required Date Time}) = 0 Then
    (
        If Hour({?Required Date Time}) = 0 Then
        (
            Date({?Required Date Time}) = Date({Orders.Ship
Date});
        )
        Else
            {?Required Date Time} = DateAdd("S", -
Second({Orders.Ship Date}),DateAdd("N", -
Minute({Orders.Ship Date}),{Orders.Ship Date}));
    )
    Else
        {?Required Date Time} = DateAdd("S", -
Second({Orders.Ship Date}),{Orders.Ship Date});

)
Else
```

$$\{?\text{Required Date Time}\} = \{\text{Orders.Ship Date}\};$$

4. Save and close the formula.

5. Refresh the report, when prompted enter the date with a time of 00:00:00.

The report will display all records for the day, regardless of their time.

Make a note of an hour value, preferably with more than one record.

6. Refresh the report, and when prompted enter the date with the hour value just noted and remaining time of 00:00.

The report will display all records for the day, at that hour, regardless of rest of their time value.

Make a note of a minute value, preferably with more than one record.

7. Refresh the report, when prompted, enter the date with the hour and minute value just noted and a seconds value of 00.

The report will display all records for the day, at that hour and minute, regardless of their second value.

Make a note of the second value.

8. Finally, refresh the report and enter the full DateTime value for a direct comparison.

The report will display all records which fully match.

Date Range Presets in Parameters and Titles

Setting up reports with preset date ranges has several advantages. It allows users to create easily comparable datasets and standardises the entire reporting process, as well as removing the possibility of user error when entering actual date ranges manually for reports.

But one of the main benefits of regulated date ranges is that they can be easily scheduled for automated distribution.

1. Create an optional string parameter called "Date Range Presets" with the following input list:

    "Last Full Month"
    "Month To Date"
    "Last Full Week"
    "Week To Date"
    "Yesterday"
    "Last 7 Days"
    "Last 14 Days"
    "Last 28 Days"

2. Save and close the parameter.

3. Create a formula called "Date (no time)" and enter the date field you wish to filter on. Save and close the formula.

4. Open the Record Selection Formula Editor and enter the following code to associate the parameter selection with the appropriate date range:

```
If HasValue({?Date Range Presets}) = False Then
(
        True
)
Else
(
```

```
Select {?Date Range Presets}
Case "Last Full Month":
        {@Date (no time)} In LastFullMonth
Case "Month To Date":
        {@Date (no time)} In MONTHToDate
Case "Last Full Week":
        {@Date (no time)} In
        Minimum(LastFullWeek) + 1 To
        Maximum(LastFullWeek) + 1
Case "Week To Date":
        {@Date (no time)} In
        Maximum(LastFullWeek) + 2 to Today
Case "Yesterday":
        {@Date (no time)} >= Today - 1
Case "Last 7 Days":
        {@Date (no time)} >= Today - 7
Case "Last 14 Days":
        {@Date (no time)} >= Today - 14
Case "Last 28 Days":
        {@Date (no time)} >= Today - 28
)
```

5. Save and close the formula.

6. Preview the report.

The report will prompt for a date range and supply the list from Step 1 to choose from.

To display the dates used as a result of the parameter choice in a report title the following formula is needed to identify the minimum and maximum dates for the selected range:

7. Create a formula called "Title Date" and enter the following code:

```
If HasValue({?Date Range Presets}) = False Then
        ToText(Minimum({GetAgentSearchStatsReport;1.
        Date}),"dd-MMM-yyyy") & " To " &
```

```
        ToText(Maximum({GetAgentSearchStatsReport;1.
        Date}),"dd-MMM-yyyy")
Else
(
        Select {?Date Range Presets}
        Case "Last Full Month":
                ToText(Minimum(lastfullmonth),"dd-MMM-
                yyyy") & " To " &
                ToText(Maximum(lastfullmonth),"dd-MMM-
                yyyy")
        Case "Month To Date":
                ToText(Minimum(monthtodate),"dd-MMM-
                yyyy") & " To " &
                ToText(Maximum(monthtodate),"dd-MMM-
                yyyy")
        Case "Last Full Week":
                ToText(Minimum(lastfullweek)+1,"dd-MMM-
                yyyy") & " To " &
                ToText(Maximum(lastfullweek)+1,"dd-
                MMM-yyyy")
        Case "Week To Date":
                ToText(Maximum(lastfullweek)+2,"dd-
                MMM-yyyy") & " To " & ToText(Today,"dd-
                MMM-yyyy")
        Case "Yesterday":
                ToText( Today -1,"dd-MMM-yyyy")
        Case "Last 7 Days":
                ToText( Today - 7,"dd-MMM-yyyy") & " To "
                & ToText(Today,"dd-MMM-yyyy")
        Case "Last 14 Days":
                ToText( Today - 14,"dd-MMM-yyyy") & " To
                " & ToText(Today,"dd-MMM-yyyy")
        Case "Last 28 Days":
                ToText( Today - 28,"dd-MMM-yyyy") & " To
                " & ToText(Today,"dd-MMM-yyyy")
        Default:
                ToText( Today -1,"dd-MMM-yyyy")
)
```

8. Save and close the formula.

9. Insert the formula into the report header and refresh the report.

The report will now display the date range used by the report.

Instance Refreshing Warning

If the above solution is to be used in reports distributed via Infoview and/or CMC, further work maybe required.

At the time of writing, drilling down on a report, or even printing it, can cause a report instance to re-evaluate contents based on the parameters it was originally run with. As date ranges are dynamically generated, a report run last week with a "Week To Date" parameter will show as being empty if inadvertently refreshed this week.

In order to preserve the report's integrity, the date ranges must be generated based on the date that the data was initially loaded.

To do this the Record Selection formula must check the date the database information was loaded into the report instance with the current date on which the report is being viewed.

If the data date is less than the date upon which the refresh has happened, then all date range calculations should be made using the data load date.

10. Open the Record Selection Formula Editor and replace the code with the following to make it dependant on the data date:

```
If HasValue({?Date Range Presets}) = False Then
(
   True
)
Else
(
```

```
If Today > DataDate then
(
    Select {?Date Range Presets}
    Case "Last Full Month":
            {@Date (no time)} In [DateAdd("M", -1,
            DateSerial(Year(DataDate),
            Month(DataDate), 1)) To DateAdd("D", -1,
            DateSerial(Year(DataDate),
            Month(DataDate), 1))]
    Case "Month To Date":
            {@Date (no time)} In
            [DateSerial(Year(DataDate),
            Month(DataDate), 1) To DataDate]
    Case "Last Full Week":
            {@Date (no time)} In [(DataDate-
            (DayOfWeek(DataDate,crMONDAY))-6) To
            DataDate-
            (DayOfWeek(DataDate,crMONDAY))]
    Case "Week To Date":
            {@Date (no time)} In [DataDate-
            (DayOfWeek(DataDate,crMONDAY))+1 To
            DataDate]
    Case "Yesterday":
            {@Date (no time)} >= (Today - 1) - (Today-
            DataDate)
    Case "Last 7 Days":
            {@Date (no time)} >= (Today - 7) - (Today-
            DataDate)
    Case "Last 14 Days":
            {@Date (no time)} >= (Today - 14) - (Today-
            DataDate)
    Case "Last 28 Days":
            {@Date (no time)} >= (Today - 28) - (Today-
            DataDate)
)
Else
(
    Select {?Date Range Presets}
```

```
            Case "Last Full Month":
                    {@Date (no time)} In LastFullMonth
            Case "Month To Date":
                    {@Date (no time)} In MonthToDate
            Case "Last Full Week":
                    {@Date (no time)} In
                    Minimum(LastFullWeek) + 1 to
                    Maximum(LastFullWeek) + 1
            Case "Week To Date":
                    {@Date (no time)} In
                    Maximum(LastFullWeek) + 2 to Today
            Case "Yesterday":
                    {@Date (no time)} >= Today - 1
            Case "Last 7 Days":
                    {@Date (no time)} >= Today - 7
            Case "Last 14 Days":
                    {@Date (no time)} >= Today - 14
            Case "Last 28 Days":
                    {@Date (no time)} >= Today - 28
        )
    )
```

11. Save and close the formula.

12. Open the formula called "Title Date" and replace the content with the following code:

```
If HasValue({?Date Range Presets}) = False Then
        ToText(Minimum({GetAgentSearchStatsReport;1.
        Date}),"dd-MMM-yyyy") & " To " &
        ToText(Maximum({GetAgentSearchStatsReport;1.
        Date}),"dd-MMM-yyyy")
Else
(
    If Today > DataDate then
    (
        Select {?Date Range Presets}
        Case "Last Full Month":
```

```
                ToText(DateAdd("M", -1,
                DateSerial(Year(DataDate),
                Month(DataDate), 1)),"dd-MMM-yyyy") & "
                To " & ToText(DateAdd("D", -1,
                DateSerial(Year(DataDate),
                Month(DataDate), 1)),"dd-MMM-yyyy")
        Case "Month To Date":
                ToText(DateSerial(Year(DataDate),
                Month(DataDate), 1),"dd-MMM-yyyy") & "
                To " & ToText(DataDate,"dd-MMM-yyyy")
        Case "Last Full Week":
                ToText((DataDate-
                (DayOfWeek(DataDate,crMONDAY))-
                6),"dd-MMM-yyyy") & " To " &
                ToText(DataDate-
                (DayOfWeek(DataDate,crMONDAY)),"dd-
                MMM-yyyy")
        Case "Week To Date":
                ToText(DataDate-
                (DayOfWeek(DataDate,crMONDAY))+1,"dd
                -MMM-yyyy") & " To " &
                ToText(DataDate,"dd-MMM-yyyy")
        Case "Yesterday":
                ToText( DataDate -1,"dd-MMM-yyyy")
        Case "Last 7 Days":
                ToText(DataDate-7,"dd-MMM-yyyy") & " To
                " & ToText(DataDate,"dd-MMM-yyyy")
        Case "Last 14 Days":
                ToText(DataDate - 14,"dd-MMM-yyyy") & "
                To " & ToText(DataDate,"dd-MMM-yyyy")
        Case "Last 28 Days":
                ToText(DataDate  - 28,"dd-MMM-yyyy") & "
                To " & ToText(DataDate,"dd-MMM-yyyy")

    )
    Else
    (
        Select {?Date Range Presets}
```

```
Case "Last Full Month":
        ToText(Minimum(lastfullmonth),"dd-MMM-
        yyyy") & " To " &
        ToText(Maximum(lastfullmonth),"dd-MMM-
        yyyy")
Case "Month To Date":
        ToText(Minimum(monthtodate),"dd-MMM-
        yyyy") & " To " &
        ToText(Maximum(monthtodate),"dd-MMM-
        yyyy")
Case "Last Full Week":
        ToText(Minimum(lastfullweek)+1,"dd-MMM-
        yyyy") & " To " &
        ToText(Maximum(lastfullweek)+1,"dd-
        MMM-yyyy")
Case "Week To Date":
        ToText(Maximum(lastfullweek)+2,"dd-
        MMM-yyyy") & " To " & ToText(Today,"dd-
        MMM-yyyy")
Case "Yesterday":
        ToText( Today -1,"dd-MMM-yyyy")
Case "Last 7 Days":
        ToText( Today - 7,"dd-MMM-yyyy") & " To "
        & ToText(Today,"dd-MMM-yyyy")
Case "Last 14 Days":
        ToText( Today - 14,"dd-MMM-yyyy") & " To
        " & ToText(Today,"dd-MMM-yyyy")
Case "Last 28 Days":
        ToText( Today - 28,"dd-MMM-yyyy") & " To
        " & ToText(Today,"dd-MMM-yyyy")
Default:
        ToText( Today -1,"dd-MMM-yyyy")
    )
)
```

13. Save and close the formula.

The report will now compare the current date with the date of the data held in the instance and behave accordingly when applying filters.

Random Record Selection

This is one request which is not as rare as maybe expected in reporting software.

Obviously, the standard basic requirement for a useful report is for it to contain and display accurately, all of the relevant data, but in some cases a random selection of a given number of records is required.

For example, a sample 10% of all sales for marketing follow up calls; or a 1% selection of customer satisfaction surveys on new items sold; a random selection of 5% of timesheets to assess time keeping…and so on.

Selecting random records is made easy, thanks to the Rnd Function.

However, this can give a false sense of random selection unless it is used properly.

The following report uses the Rnd Function to randomly alter the Group Order, then uses Record Count to limit the records shown.

Report Name: RandomSamples.rpt

Report Requirement: To provide a list of 10, 20 or 50 random customers for the marketing department to survey.

Report Details:

Table	Fields	Filter
Customer	Customer ID Customer Name Contact First Name Contact Last Name City Phone	Country = "USA"

NB: This report will load up all records with the Country of "USA", before selecting the random 50 records. This is something to bear in mind when dealing with large amounts of data.

1. Create a number parameter called "prmSelectNumberOfRecords" with default values of 10, 20 and 50.

2. Create a new formula called "frmRandomGroupOrder" and enter the following code:

```
Rnd();
```

3. Save and close the formula.

4. Sort the report based on the formula (Ascending or Descending, it doesn't matter in this case.).

5. Refresh the report a few times and note how the report order changes each time.

6. In the Suppress Formula Editor for the Detail Section enter the following code:

```
If RecordNumber  > {?prmSelectNumberOfRecords} Then
    True
Else
    False;
```

7. Save the formula and refresh the report several times, selecting a different number of records to display each time when prompted.

The report will display the correct number of random records every time.

NB: This is a runtime calculation in the same way as filtering by groups, and the same rules apply - any summaries must be done via running totals.

Two Dimensional Arrays

A two dimensional array is an array that contains other arrays, it may sound confusing, but they are a powerful tool and used often in traditional programming.

At the time of writing, Crystal Reports does not support two dimensional arrays through the traditional syntax. However, the Split Function can be used with a standard array to create something with the same functionality.

Two dimensional arrays allow a report writer to build a collection of main items, such as sales reps, and for each of those build a collection of item belonging to them, like all the customers for each sales rep.

Report Name: TwoDimensionalArrays.rpt

Report Requirement: Populate an array with customers and the dates on which they placed an order.

Report Details:

Table(s)	Fields
Customer	Customer Name
Orders	Date Ordered

Additional Setup:

Suppress every section except the Report Footer.

1. Create a formula called "frmBuild2DimArry" and enter the following code:

```
global stringVar Array astr2DimArray;

Local numberVar x;
```

```
IF recordnumber = 1 then
(
    Redim Preserve astr2DimArray[1];
    astr2DimArray[ubound(astr2DimArray)] :=
{Customer.Customer Name} & "#" & {Orders.Order Date}
& "#";
)
Else
(
    For x := 1 to ubound(astr2DimArray) Do
    (
        If {Customer.Customer Name} =
        mid(astr2DimArray[x],1,
        instr(astr2DimArray[x],"#")-1) Then

                astr2DimArray[x] := astr2DimArray[x] &
                {Orders.Order Date} & "#"

         else If x = ubound(astr2DimArray) then
         (
                Redim Preserve
        astr2DimArray[ubound(astr2DimArray)+1];

                astr2DimArray[ubound(astr2DimArray)] :=
                {Customer.Customer Name} & "#" &
                {Orders.Order Date} & "#";
        );

     );
    astr2DimArray[ubound(astr2DimArray)];
);
```

2. Save and close the formula and insert it into the Detail Section.

This is a basic array, except for the Order Dates being concatenated to the end of the customer names and separated with a "#".

The first position in astr2DimArray is always the Customer Name, and anything after that is their Order Dates.

As the contents of astr2DimArray are separated using "#", each element can now be identified and displayed in much the same way as a traditional array.

3. Create a dynamic string parameter based on the Customer Name field called "prmViewDates".

4. Create a formula called "frmDisplayOneCustomer" and enter the following code:

```
evaluateafter({@frmBuild2DimArry});

global stringVar Array astr2DimArray;

Local numberVar x;
Local numberVar y;
Local stringVar strDisplay;

For x := 1 to ubound(astr2DimArray) Do
(
        If {?prmViewDates} = mid(astr2DimArray[x],1,
        instr(astr2DimArray[x],"#")-1) Then
        (
                strDisplay := mid(astr2DimArray[x],1,
                instr(astr2DimArray[x],"#")-1) &
                " Ordered on these Dates: " & chr(13);

                strDisplay := strDisplay &
                replace(mid(astr2DimArray[x],instr(astr2Dim
                Array[x],"#")+1), "#", "," & chr(13));
        );
);

strDisplay;
```

5. Save and close the formula and insert it in the Report Footer.

6. Preview the report.

When prompted, select a Company Name. The report will list all the Order Date in the report.

This exercise could have been realised with a much simpler, basic report. But the same coding methods can be used to provide summary lists at the end of reports (without resorting to a sub report) or to highlight records of a particular type.

NB: A string variable is not an infinite length and as a result, this solution may not be suitable for cases where each array element may end up with a large amount of data.

Ranking Formula

Displaying the top (or bottom) few records in a report is easily achieved using the built in Group Sort Expert.

To display all records but separately total the top and bottom few records requires work.

Report Name: RankingReport.rpt

Report Requirement: Allow the top and bottom three records to be totalled separately based on number of orders..

.

Report Details:

Table(s)	Fields	Groups
Customers	Customer ID	Customer ID
	Customer Name	
Orders	Order ID	

Additional Setup:

Insert a Distinct Count based on the Order ID into the Group Footer.

Use the Group Sort Expert to create a Top N sort, 'Where N is:' 1000, 'Based on' the Distinct Count created above.

This will order the result in the report to enable easy identification of the top and bottom records.

1. Create a formula called "frmTotalsArray" and enter the following code:

```
Global numbervar array aintTotalsArray;
Global numbervar  t;
```

```
If t = 0 then
(
        t := 1;

        redim preserve aintTotalsArray[t];

         aintTotalsArray[t] := DistinctCount
        ({Orders.Order_ID}, {Customer.Customer_ID});
)
Else
(
        t := t + 1;

        redim preserve aintTotalsArray[t];

        aintTotalsArray[t] := DistinctCount
        ({Orders.Order_ID}, {Customer.Customer_ID});
);
```

2. Save and close the formula and insert it in the Group Footer.

This code creates an array that can be used to identify and total the top
and bottom three totals.

NB: Ties between totals are treated as one position.

3. Create a formula called "frmBottom3Total" and add the following
    code:

```
EvaluateAfter ({@frmTotalsArray});

Global numbervar array aintTotalsArray;
Global numbervar intBottom3Total;
Global numbervar intLastrecord;

local numbervar k;
local numbervar f;
```

```
        k := 1;

        intLastrecord := aintTotalsArray[ubound(aintTotalsArray)];

        intBottom3Total := intLastrecord;

        For f := ubound(aintTotalsArray)-2 to 1 step -1 do
        (

            If k < 3 then
            (
                    If aintTotalsArray[f] > intLastrecord Then
                    (
                            intLastrecord := aintTotalsArray[f];
                            intBottom3Total := intBottom3Total +
                            aintTotalsArray[f];
                            k := k + 1;
                    )
                    Else If aintTotalsArray[f] = intLastrecord  Then
                    (
                            intBottom3Total := intBottom3Total +
                            aintTotalsArray[f];
                    );
            )
        );

        intBottom3Total;
```

4. Close and save the formula and insert it into the Report Footer.

5. Create a formula called "frmTop3Total" and add the following
    code:

```
        EvaluateAfter ({@frmTotalsArray});

        Global numbervar array aintTotalsArray;
        Global numbervar intTop3Total;
```

```
Global numbervar intLastrecord;

local numbervar k;
local numbervar f;

k := 1;

intLastrecord := aintTotalsArray[1];

intTop3Total := intLastrecord;

For f := 2 to ubound(aintTotalsArray) do
(
        If k < 3 then
        (
                If aintTotalsArray[f] < intLastrecord Then
                (
                        intLastrecord := aintTotalsArray[f];
                        intTop3Total := intTop3Total +
                        aintTotalsArray[f];
                        k := k + 1;
                )
                Else If aintTotalsArray[f] = intLastrecord
                Then
                (
                        intTop3Total := intTop3Total +
                aintTotalsArray[f];
                );
        )
);

intTop3Total;
```

6. Close and save the formula and insert it into the Report Footer.

7. Preview the report.

The report will total the top and bottom three records separately.

Appendix A: Code Listings / Quick Guide

A lot of the formula code within the exercises in Section One is split up to enable a step by step break down of the points being illustrated.

For ease of reference, the code is listed here in its entirety. This section can be used for future reference after completing the Section One tutorials.

Report Name: String_uses.rpt

frmFullName:

```
"Employee Full Name: " & {Employee.First Name} & " " &
{Employee.Last Name};
```

frmReportTitle:

```
"List Of Employees" & CHRW(13) & "Report Run: " & PrintDate;
```

frmRemoveCode:

```
Replace(Mid({Employee.Home Phone},instr({Employee.Home
Phone},")") + 1),"-"," ");
```

frmLastFive:

```
Right({Employee.SSN},5);
```

frmFullName(second version):

```
"Employee Full Name:" & ReplicateString ("_",20 - Len(
{Employee.First Name} & {Employee.Last Name})) &
{Employee.First Name} & " " & {Employee.Last Name};
```

frmDifferentCase:

```
ProperCase("EMPLOYEE FULL NAME: ") &
UpperCase({Employee.First Name}) & " " &
LowerCase({Employee.Last Name})
```

Report Name: Maths_Examples.rpt

frmVAT:

```
{Orders_Detail.Unit Price} * 0.175;
```

frmWithVAT:

```
{Orders_Detail.Unit Price} + ({Orders_Detail.Unit Price} * 0.175);
```

frmLineTotalVAT:

```
({Orders_Detail.Unit Price} + ({Orders_Detail.Unit Price} *
0.175)) * {Orders_Detail.Quantity};
```

frmAverageUnitCost:

```
Sum ({@frmLineTotalVAT}, {Orders_Detail.Order ID}) / Sum
({Orders_Detail.Quantity}, {Orders_Detail.Order ID});
```

frmAverageBeforeVAT:

```
Sum({Orders_Detail.Unit Price}, {Orders_Detail.Order ID})  /
Count({Orders_Detail.Product ID}, {Orders_Detail.Order ID});
```

Report Name: Percentage_Example.rpt

frmOnTime:

```
If {Orders.Ship Date} < {Orders.Required Date} Then
   1
Else
   0;
```

frmPercentOntime:

```
(Sum({@frmOnTime}, {Orders.Customer ID})
/
Count({Orders.Order ID}, {Orders.Customer ID})) * 100;
```

frmPercentOverall:

```
(Sum({@frmOnTime})
/
Count({Orders.Order ID}) * 100;
```

frmAlwaysRoundUp:

```
numberVar intNumber := 5.5;

If (Truncate(intNumber,0) + 0.5) <> intNumber Then
        Round(intNumber)
Else If Remainder(Truncate(intNumber,0),2) > 0 Then
        RoundUp(intNumber)
Else
        Truncate(intNumber,0);
```

Report Name: Conversion_Examples.rpt

frmTextEmployeeID:

```
ToText({Orders.Customer ID},0,"");
```

frmNumberEmployeeID:

```
ToNumber({@TextEmployeeID});
```

frmNumberEmployeeID(second version):

```
If IsNumeric({Orders.Customer ID}) = True Then
        ToNumber({@TextEmployeeID});
```

frmCreateDate:

```
stringVar strDateString := "29/08/2009";

Date(strDateString);
```

frmCreateDate(second version):

```
stringVar DateString := "29/08/2009";

If IsDate(DateString) Then
        Date(DateString);
```

frmCreateDateTime:

```
stringVar DateTimeString := "29/08/2009 23:59:59";

If IsDateTime(DateTimeString) Then
        DateTime(DateTimeString);
```

frmstrAddressarray:

```
stringVar array strAddressarray :=
Split({Employee_Addresses.Address1}," ");

strAddressarray[1];
```

Report Name: Date_Functions.rpt

frmRequiredYear:

```
Year({Orders.Required Date});
```

frmRequiredMonth:

```
Month({Orders.Required Date});
```

frmRequiredDay:

Day({Orders.Required Date});

frmRequiredDate:

Date({@frmRequiredYear},{@frmRequiredMonth},{@frm
RequiredDay});

frmRandomTime:

DateTime({@frmRequiredYear},{@frmRequiredMonth},{
@frmRequiredDay}, truncate(Rnd() * 24), truncate(Rnd()
* 60), truncate(Rnd() * 60));

frmRequiredDate(Second Version):

numberVar intMonth := Truncate(Rnd() * 15);

Date({@RequiredYear}, intMonth, {@RequiredDay});

frmRequiredDate(Third Version):

numberVar intMonth := Truncate(Rnd() * 15);

If IsDate(ToText ({@RequiredYear},0,"") & "," & ToText
(intMonth,0, "") & "," & ToText({@RequiredDay},0,""))
Then
        Date({@RequiredYear}, intMonth,
    {@RequiredDay})
Else
        Date(0,0,0);

Selection formula:

{?prmSelectAMonth} = MonthName({@RequiredMonth});

frmReportTitle:

"Orders Report for The Month Of " &
MonthName({@RequiredMonth},True)

frmRequiredDayName:

stringVar array strWeekDays := ["Sunday","Monday",
"Tuesday", "Wednesday", "Thursday", "Friday",
"Saturday"];

If DayOfWeek({@RandomDate}) > 0 Then
        strWeekDays[DayOfWeek({@RandomDate})]
Else
        "Invalid Date";

Report Name: Date_Comparisons.rpt

frmQuickDays:

{Orders.Ship Date}-{Orders.Order Date};

frmDiffDays:

DateDiff("d",{Orders.Order Date},{Orders.Ship Date});

frmDiffSeconds:

DateDiff("s",{Orders.Order Date},{Orders.Ship Date});

frmDateOffSet:

DateAdd("D",2,{Orders.Ship Date});

frmDateOffSet(Second Version):

DateAdd("M",2,{Orders.Ship Date});

frmDateOffSet(third Version):

```
DateAdd("Q",-2,{Orders.Ship Date});
```

frmNestedDateOffSet:

```
DateAdd("M",1,DateAdd("D",3,{Orders.Ship Date}));
```

Report Name: Date_Ranges.rpt

frmTestDate:

```
numberVar intDay := Truncate(Rnd() * Day(Today)+1);
numberVar intMonth := Truncate (Rnd () *
Month(Today)+1);
numberVar intYear := Truncate (Rnd () * 2);

Date(ToText(intDay,0,"") & "/" &  ToText(intMonth,0,"") &
"/" & ToText(Year(Today)-intYear,0,""));
```

frmWithinLastWeek:

```
If {@frmTestDate} In Last7Days Then
        "Within One Week"
Else
        "Not Within One Week";
```

frmWithinLastFullmonth:

```
If {@frmTestDate} In LastFullMonth Then
        "Within Last Full Month"
Else
        "Not Within Last Full Month";
```

frmWithinThismonth:

```
If {@frmTestDate} In MonthToDate Then
        "Within This Month"
Else
        "Not Within This Month";
```

frmWithinThisYear:

```
If {@frmTestDate} In YearToDate Then
        "Within This Year"
Else
        "Not Within This Year";
```

frmWithin2FullMonths:

```
If {@frmTestDate} In DateAdd("M",-
1,Minimum(LastFullMonth)) To Maximum(LastFullMonth)
Then
        "Within Last Two Full Months"
Else
        "Not Within Last Two Full Months";
```

Report Name: Variable_uses.rpt

frmStringVariables:

```
stringVar StringTestVariable;

StringTestVariable := "Different Literal Value";

StringTestVariable := StringTestVariable & " and the Field
Courier Website: ";

StringTestVariable := StringTestVariable &
{Orders.Courier Website};

"Not The Variable";

StringTestVariable := UPPERCase(StringTestVariable);

ProperCase(StringTestVariable);

StringTestVariable := ToText({Orders.Employee ID},0,"");
```

```
        StringTestVariable := "Employee ID: " &
{Orders.Employee ID};
```

frmIntTests:

```
        numberVar IntTestVariable;

        numberVar IntTestVariable := 72;

        IntTestVariable := 3;

        IntTestVariable := 2 * 9.55;

        IntTestVariable := (2 + 9) * 3;

        IntTestVariable := 7/4;

        IntTestVariable := IntTestVariable * 8;

        IntTestVariable := SQR(IntTestVariable);

        Truncate(IntTestVariable);
```

frmDateTests:

```
        datetimeVar DteTestVariable;
        dateVar DateTestVariable;

        DteTestVariable := #23/01/2010#;

        DteTestVariable := #23/01/2010 12:00:00#;

        DateTestVariable :=  #23/01/2010 12:00:00#;
```

frmDateTests(Second Version):

```
        datetimeVar DteTestVariable;
```

```
dateVar DateTestVariable;

DteTestVariable := #23/01/2010#;

DteTestVariable := #23/01/2010 12:00:00#;

DateTestVariable := Date(#23/01/2010 12:00:00#);
```

frmBlnTests:

```
booleanVar BlnTestVariable;

BlnTestVariable := True;

BlnTestVariable := 2 = 2;

BlnTestVariable := 2 = 3;

BlnTestVariable := {Orders.Ship Date} >=
{Orders.Required Date};
```

Report Name: Variables_Between_Formulas.rpt

frmSetupVariable:

```
Global numberVar IntVariable := 5;
```

frmShowVariable:

```
Global numberVar IntVariable;
```

frmShowVariable(Second Version):

```
Global numberVar IntVariable;

IntVariable := IntVariable + 5;
```

frmSetupVariable(Second Version):

```
Global numberVar IntVariable := 5;

IntVariable := 10;
```

Report Name: Variables_and_subreports.rpt

frmSetupVariable:

```
Shared numberVar IntCustomerOrders := DistinctCount
({Orders.OrderID}, {Orders.CustomerID});
```

frmuseVariable:

```
Shared numberVar IntCustomerOrders;

(IntCustomerOrders / DistinctCount ({Orders.OrderID},
{Orders.Country})) * 100;
```

frmSetupVariable(Second Version):

```
Shared numberVar IntCustomerOrders := DistinctCount
({Orders.OrderID}, {Orders.CustomerID});

Shared stringVar CustomerName :=
{Orders.CustomerID};
```

frmuseVariable(Second Version):

```
Shared stringVar CustomerName;
Shared numberVar IntCustomerOrders;

CustomerName & "  " & ToText((IntCustomerOrders /
DistinctCount ({Orders.OrderID}, {Orders.Country})) *
100);
```

Report Name: Control_Structures.rpt

frmIfStatement:

```
If {Employees.EmployeeID} > 4 Then
        "Option 1: Employee ID 5 or more.";
```

frmIfStatement(Second Version):

```
If {Employees.EmployeeID} > 4 Then
        "Option 1: Employee ID 5 or more."
Else
        "Option 2: Employee ID less than 5.";
```

frmIfStatement(Third Version):

```
If {Employees.EmployeeID} > 4 Then
        "Option 1: Employee ID 5 or more."
Else If {Employees.EmployeeID} > 2 Then
        "Option 2: Employee ID between 2 and 5."
Else
        "Option 3: Employee ID less than 3.";
```

frmIfStatementExtended:

```
If {Employees.EmployeeID} < 5 Then
        "Option 1: Employee ID less than 5."
Else If {Employees.Title} = "Sales Representative" Then
        "Option 2: Both Conditions Met"
Else
        "Option 3: Right Employee ID, wrong Job Title.";

numberVar EmployeeID := 1000;
```

frmIfStatementExtended(Second Version):

```
If {Employees.EmployeeID} < 5 Then
        "Option 1: Employee ID less than 5."
Else If {Employees.Title} = "Sales Representative" Then
        (
```

```
        EmployeeID := EmployeeID +
{Employees.EmployeeID};
        {Employees.LastName} & " " &
ToText(EmployeeID,0,"");
)
Else
        "Option 3: Right Employee ID, wrong Job Title.";
```

frmIfBalancing(Error):

```
If {Employees.EmployeeID} > 4 Then
        {Employees.EmployeeID}
Else
        {Employees.Title};
```

frmIfBalancing(Correct):

```
If {Employees.EmployeeID} > 4 Then
        ToText({Employees.EmployeeID},0,"")
Else
        {Employees.Title};
```

frmIfCheat(Error):

```
numberVar numEmployeeID := {Employees.EmployeeID};
stringVar strEmployeeName := {Employees.LastName};

If {Employees.EmployeeID} > 4 Then
(
        numEmployeeID := numEmployeeID + 1000;
)
Else
(
        strEmployeeName := {Employees.LastName} & ", "
        & {Employees.FirstName};
);

strEmployeeName & " " & ToText(numEmployeeID,0,"");
```

frmIfCheat(Correct):

```
numberVar numEmployeeID := {Employees.EmployeeID};
stringVar strEmployeeName := {Employees.LastName};

If {Employees.EmployeeID} > 4 Then
(
        numEmployeeID := numEmployeeID + 1000;
        "Bit Of Text To Fool Crystal Reports";
)
Else
(
        strEmployeeName := {Employees.LastName} & ", "
        & {Employees.FirstName};
 );

strEmployeeName & " " & ToText(numEmployeeID,0,"");
```

frmIfCheat(Second Correct Version):

```
numberVar numEmployeeID := {Employees.EmployeeID};
stringVar strEmployeeName := {Employees.LastName};

If {Employees.EmployeeID} > 4 Then
(
        EmployeeID := EmployeeID + 1000;
)
Else
(
        EmployeeName := {Employees.LastName} & ", " &
        {Employees.FirstName};
        1;
 );

strEmployeeName & " " & ToText(numEmployeeID,0,"");
```

Report Name: Nested_If_Statement.rpt

Record selection formula:

```
If {Product.Color} In {?prmcolor} Then
        True
Else If {Product.Size} In {?prmSize} Then
        True
Else If {Product.Supplier ID} In {?prmSupplier} Then
        True
Else
        False;
```

Record selection formula(Second Version):

```
If {Product.Color} = "Black" Then
(
        If {Product.Size} In {?prmSize} Then
                True
        Else If {Product.Supplier ID} In {?prmSupplier}
        Then
                True
        Else
                False;
)
Else
(
        False
);
```

Record selection formula(Third Version):

```
If {Product.Color} = "Black" Then
(
        False;
)
Else
(
        If {Product.Size} In {?prmSize} Then
```

```
                        True
                Else If {Product.Supplier ID} In {?prmSupplier}
                Then
                        True
                Else
                        False;
        );
```

Report Name: select_Example.rpt

frmCountryByColor:

```
        If {Customer.Country} = "USA" Then
                crRed
        Else If {Customer.Country} = "Canada" Then
                crBlue
        Else If {Customer.Country} = "England" Then
                crGreen
        Else If {Customer.Country} = "Australia" Then
                crGray
        Else If {Customer.Country} = "Brazil" Then
                crYellow
        Else If {Customer.Country} = "France" Then
                crPurple
        Else
                crWhite;
```

frmCountryByColor(Second Version):

```
        Select{Customer.Country}
        Case "USA":
                crRed
        Case "Canada":
                crBlue
        Case "England":
                crGreen
        Case  "Australia":
                crGray
```

```
Case  "Brazil":
        crYellow
Case "France":
        crPurple
Default:
        crWhite;
```

frmIIf_Formula:

```
IIf({Customer.Country} = "USA", crBlue, crBlack);
```

frmIIf_Formula(Second Version):

```
IIf({Customer.Country} = "USA", crBlue,
IIf({Customer.Country} = "Canada", crRed, crBlack));
```

frmSwitch:

```
Switch({Customer.Last Year's Sales} > 100000, "Gold
Customer",
{Customer.Last Year's Sales} > 20000, "Silver Customer",
True, "Standard Customer");
```

frmChoose:

```
Choose(DayOfWeek({Orders.Order Date}), "Sunday",
"Monday", "Tuesday", "Wednesday", "Thursday",
"Friday", "Saturday");
```

Report Name: Loop_Examples.rpt

frmSpacesInStrFirstSentence:

```
numberVar x := 1;
numberVar NumberOfSpaces := 0;

While {Product_Type.Description}[x] <> "." Do
(
```

```
            If {Product_Type.Description}[x] = " " Then
                  NumberOfSpaces := NumberOfSpaces + 1;


            x := x + 1;
      );


      NumberOfSpaces;
```

frmStrFirstSentence:

```
      numberVar y := 1;
      stringVar StrFirstSentence:= "";

      While {Product_Type.Description}[y] <> "." Do
      (
            StrFirstSentence:= StrFirstSentence &
            {Product_Type.Description}[y];

            y := y + 1;
      );

      StrFirstSentence;
```

frmStrFirstSentence(Second Version):

```
      numberVar y := 0;
      stringVar StrFirstSentence:= "";

      Do
      (
            y := y + 1;

            StrFirstSentence:= StrFirstSentence &
            {Product_Type.Description}[y];

      )While {Product_Type.Description}[y] <> ".";

      StrFirstSentence;
```

frmListVowels:

```
numberVar z;
stringVar VowelList := "";

For z := 1 To 20 Do
(
    If {Product_Type.Description}[z] in ["a","e","i","o","u"]
Then
    (
        VowelList := VowelList &
{Product_Type.Description}[z]
    );
);

VowelList;
```

frmListVowels(Second Variation):

```
numberVar z;
stringVar VowelList := "";

For z := 1 To 20 STEP 2 Do
(
    If {Product_Type.Description}[z] in ["a","e","i","o","u"]
Then
    (
        VowelList := VowelList &
{Product_Type.Description}[z]
    );
);

VowelList;
```

frmFirst10Vowels:

```
numberVar z;
```

```
stringVar VowelList := "";

For z := 1 To 200000 Do
(
   If {Product_Type.Description}[z] in ["a","e","i","o","u"]
Then
   (
      VowelList := VowelList &
{Product_Type.Description}[z]
   );
);

VowelList;
```

frmFirst10Vowels(Second Variation):

```
numberVar z;
stringVar VowelList := "";

For z := 1 To 200000  Do
(
   If Len ({Product_Type.Description}) < z Then
       Exit For;

   If {Product_Type.Description}[z] in ["a","e","i","o","u"]
Then
   (
      VowelList := VowelList &
{Product_Type.Description}[z]
   );
);

VowelList;
```

frmLettersUpToK:

```
numberVar v := 1;
stringVar LettersUpToK:= "";
```

```
While {Product_Type.Description}[v] <> "k" Do
(
        LettersUpToK:= LettersUpToK &
        {Product_Type.Description}[v];

        v := v + 1;
);

LettersUpToK;
```

frmLettersUpToK(Second Variation):

```
numberVar v := 1;
stringVar LettersUpToK:= "";

While {Product_Type.Description}[v] <> "k" Do
(
        LettersUpToK:= LettersUpToK &
        {Product_Type.Description}[v];

        v := v + 1;

        If v > Len({Product_Type.Description}) Then
                Exit While;
);

LettersUpToK;
```

Report Name: array_Usage.rpt

frmUpdatearray:

```
stringVar array astrCountry;
numberVar array aintStaffTotal;

Local numberVar x;
Local numberVar y;
```

```
If {Employee_Addresses.Country} In astrCountry Then
(
        For x:=1 To UBound(astrCountry)  do
        (
                If {Employee_Addresses.Country} =
                astrCountry[x] Then
                        y:=x;
        );

        aintStaffTotal[y] := aintStaffTotal[y] + 1;
)
Else
(
        Redim Preserve
        astrCountry[UBound(astrCountry)+1];
        Redim Preserve
        aintStaffTotal[UBound(aintStaffTotal)+1];

        astrCountry[UBound(astrCountry)] :=
        {Employee_Addresses.Country};

        aintStaffTotal[UBound(aintStaffTotal)] := 1;
);
```

frmDisplayCountryarray:

```
EvaluateAfter ({@frmUpdatearray});

stringVar array astrCountry;
numberVar z;

stringVar strDisplayCountry;
astrCountry[1] := "Country";

For z := 1 To UBound(astrCountry) Do
(
```

```
                strDisplayCountry := strDisplayCountry &
                astrCountry[z] & Chr(13);
        );

        strDisplayCountry;
```

frmDisplayStaffTotalarray:

```
        EvaluateAfter ({@frmUpdatearray});

        numberVar array aintStaffTotal;

        numberVar t;

        stringVar strDisplayStaff;
        aintStaffTotal[1] := "Number Of Staff" & Chr(13);

        For t := 1 To UBound(aintStaffTotal) Do
        (
                strDisplayStaff := strDisplayStaff &
                ToText(aintStaffTotal[t],0,"") & Chr(13);
        );

        strDisplayStaff;
```

Report Name: Range_Examples.rpt

frmDateTitleRange:

```
        "Hired From " & Minimum({?prmHireDateSelection}) & "
        To " & Maximum({?Hire Date selection});
```

Record selection:

```
        If {Employee.Hire Date} In {?prmHireDateSelection} Then
                True
        Else
                False;
```

frmPositionAbbreviation:

```
{Employee.Position}[1 To 9];
```

Null Example:

```
StringVar strFirstName := " ";
StringVar strLastName := " ";

If isnull({Customer.First Name}) = false then
(
        strFirstName := {Customer.First Name};
);

If isnull({Customer.Last Name}) = false then
(
        strLastName := {Customer.Last Name};
);

strFirstName & " " & strLastName;
```

Report Name: selection_Formula.rpt

Record selection:

```
{Customer.Country} In {?One Or More Country}
And
Select {Customer.Country}
Case "USA":
        {Customer.Last Year's Sales} > 65000
Case "England":
        {Customer.Last Year's Sales} > 50000
Case "France":
        {Customer.Last Year's Sales} > 45000
Case "Germany":
        {Customer.Last Year's Sales} > 35000
Default:
```

```
{Customer.Last Year's Sales} > 30000;
```

Report Name: Group_Selection.rpt

Group selection:

```
Sum ({Orders.Order Amount}, {Customer.Customer ID}) >
{Customer.Last Year's Sales};
```

Group selection(Second Version):

```
Sum ({Orders.Order Amount}, {Customer.Customer ID}) >
{Customer.Last Year's Sales}
And
Sum ({Orders.Order Amount}, {Customer.Customer ID}) <
10000;
```

Report Name: Optional_Parameters_Old.rpt

Record selection:

```
booleanVar blnInclude_Record := False;

If {?prmSelectCountry} = " NONE" Then
        blnInclude_Record := True
Else
        blnInclude_Record := ({Customer.Country} In
        {?prmSelectCountry});

If blnInclude_Record := False Then
        False
Else If {?prmSelectWord} = " NONE" Then
        blnInclude_Record := True
Else
        blnInclude_Record := ({Customer.Customer Name}
        LIKE "*" & {?prmSelectWord} & "*");

blnInclude_Record;
```

Report Name: Optional_Parameters.rpt

Record selection:

```
(not HasValue({?prmSelectCountry}) Or
{Customer.Country} in [{?prmSelectCountry}])
and
(not HasValue({?prmSelectSalesAmount}) Or
{Customer.Last Year's Sales} >
{?prmSelectSalesAmount})
and
(not HasValue({?prmSelectWord}) Or
{Customer.Customer Name} like "*" & {?prmSelectWord}
& "*");
```

frmTitleOrderAmountMinimum:

```
If HasValue({?prmSelectSalesAmount}) Then
        ToText({?prmSelectSalesAmount})
Else
        "No Minimum Price selected";
```

Report Name: DrillDown.rpt

frmDrillLevelReference:

```
DrillDownGroupLevel;
```

Font Style:

```
If DrillDownGroupLevel = 2 Then
    crBold
Else
    crRegular;
```

frmGroupNameTitle:

```
Select DrillDownGroupLevel
Case 0:
        "Country"
Case 1:
        {Customer.Country} & " Regions"
Case 2:
        {Customer.Region} & " Cities"
Case 3:
        {Customer.City} & " Customers"
Case 4:
        "Customers";
```

Report Name: Summaries.rpt

Running Total 1:

```
If {Orders.Order Amount} < 100 Then
    True
Else
    False;
```

Running Total 2:

```
If {Orders.Payment Received} = False Then
    True
Else
    False;
```

frmHandlingCharge:

```
((ToNumber(Sum({Orders.Order Amount},
{Orders.Customer ID})) /100)* 5) + Sum({Orders.Order
Amount}, {Orders.Customer ID});
```

frmOwedOrderAmounts:

```
If {Orders.Payment Received} = False Then
        {Orders.Order Amount}
```

```
Else
        0;
```

Report Name: Subreport.rpt

frmCountryList:

```
Shared stringVar array astrCountries;

Redim Preserve astrCountries[UBound(astrCountries)+1];

astrCountries[UBound(astrCountries)] :=
{Customer.Country};

astrCountries[UBound(astrCountries)];
```

Color formula:

```
If {Customer.Country} In astrCountries Then
      crGreen
Else
      crWhite;
```

Color formula 2:

```
If {?Select_Color} = "Black" Then
      crBlack
Else If {?Select_Color} = "Red" Then
      crRed
Else
      crBlue;
```

Report Name: formatting.rpt

Background formula:

```
If {?prmDisplayBlueBackground} = True Then
      Color(50, 10, 255)
```

```
            Else
                    crSilver;
```

Font formula:

```
            If {Employee.Position} = "Sales Representative" Then
                    crBoldItalic
            Else
                    crItalic;
```

Report Name: Charts.rpt
frmCustomerOrEmployee:

```
            If {?prmChartContent} = "Customer" Then
                    {Orders.Customer ID}
            Else
                    {Orders.Employee ID};
```

frmOrdersOrPaid:

```
            If {?prmChartContent2} = "Paid" Then
                    Count({Orders.Payment
                    Received},{@CustomerOrEmployee})
            Else
                    Count({Orders.Order
                    ID},{@CustomerOrEmployee});
```

frmChartMainTitle:

```
            If {?prmChartContent2} = "Orders" Then
                    "Total Of Orders By " & {?prmChartContent}
            Else
                    "Total Of Paid Orders By " & {?prmChartContent};
```

frmChartDataTitle:

```
            If {?prmChartContent2} = "Orders" Then
                    "Total Of Orders"
            Else
                    "Total Of Paid Orders"
```

Appendix B Calendar Code

Code for frmMonday at the end of the Add the data into the calendar grid section:

```
EvaluateAfter ({@frmCalendar});
Global stringVar array astrCalendar;
Local dateVar x := (

If DayOfWeek({?The First Of The Required Month},crMonday) = 1
Then
        {?The First Of The Required Month}
Else
        {?The First Of The Required Month} - DayOfWeek({?The First
        Of The Required Month},crTuesday));

Local dateVar array adteMonday := [x, x+7, x+14, x+21, x+28, x+35];

'<b>' & ToText(Day(adteMonday[1]),0,'') & '</b></br>' &
(If Day(adteMonday[1])< 7 Then
astrCalendar[Day(adteMonday[1])] & '</br>' Else  '</br>') &

'<b>' & ToText(Day(adteMonday[2]),0,'') & '</b></br>' &

astrCalendar[Day(adteMonday[2])]& '</br>' &

'<b>' & ToText(Day(adteMonday[3]),0,'') & '</b></br>' &

astrCalendar[Day(adteMonday[3])]& '</br>' &

'<b>' & ToText(Day(adteMonday[4]),0,'') & '</b></br>' &

astrCalendar[Day(adteMonday[4])]& '</br>' &

If adteMonday[5] < DateAdd('M',1,{?The First Of The Required
Month})+(7-DayOfWeek(DateAdd('M',1,{?The First Of The Required
Month})-1,crMonday)) Then
```

```
        '<b>' & ToText(Day(adteMonday[5]),0,'') & '</b></br>' &

astrCalendar[Day(adteMonday[5])]& '</br>' &

If adteMonday[6] < DateAdd('M',1,{?The First Of The Required
Month})+(7-DayOfWeek(DateAdd('M',1,{?The First Of The Required
Month})-1,crMonday)) Then
        '<b>' & ToText(Day(adteMonday[6]),0,'') & '</b></br>' &

        astrCalendar[Day(adteMonday[6])]& '</br>';
```

Code for frmPadElements in the format the report into a calendar style
grid section:

```
EvaluateAfter ({@frmCalendar});

Global stringVar array astrCalendar;

Local numberVar a;
Local numberVar b;

Local numberVar intElementSize;
Local numberVar intPadding;


For a := 1 To UBound(astrCalendar) Do
(
   intElementSize := 0;

   For b := 1 To UBound(Split(astrCalendar[a], "</br>")) Do
   (
        intElementSize :=  intElementSize +
        (RoundUp(Len(Split(astrCalendar[a], "</br>")[b])/28));
   );

   If intElementSize > intPadding Then
```

```
        intPadding := intElementSize;
);

For a := 1 To UBound(astrCalendar) Do
(
   intElementSize := 0;

   For b := 1 To UBound(Split(astrCalendar[a], "</br>")) Do
   (
        intElementSize :=  intElementSize +
        (RoundUp(Len(Split(astrCalendar[a], "</br>")[b])/28));
   );

   If intPadding > intElementSize Then
        astrCalendar[a] := astrCalendar[a] &
        ReplicateString("</br>",((intPadding) - intElementSize));
);

intPadding;
```

Code for frmMonday in the format the report into a calendar style grid section:

```
EvaluateAfter ({@frmPadElements});
Global stringVar array astrCalendar;

Local dateVar x := (
If DayOfWeek({?The First Of The Required Month},crMonday) = 1
Then
        {?The First Of The Required Month}
Else
        {?The First Of The Required Month} - DayOfWeek({?The First
        Of The Required Month},crTuesday));

Local dateVar array adteMonday := [x, x+7, x+14, x+21, x+28, x+35];
```

```
'<b><DIV ALIGN = "CENTER"> ' & ToText(Day(adteMonday[1]),0,'') &
'</DIV></b></br>' &
(If Day(adteMonday[1])< 7 Then
    astrCalendar[Day(adteMonday[1])]& '</br>'  Else
    ReplicateString('</br>', {@frmPadElements}) ) &

'<b><DIV ALIGN = "CENTER"> ' & ToText(Day(adteMonday[2]),0,'') &
'</DIV></b></br>' &
astrCalendar[Day(adteMonday[2])]& '</br>' &

'<b><DIV ALIGN = "CENTER"> ' & ToText(Day(adteMonday[3]),0,'') &
'</DIV></b></br>' &
astrCalendar[Day(adteMonday[3])]& '</br>' &

'<b><DIV ALIGN = "CENTER"> ' & ToText(Day(adteMonday[4]),0,'') &
'</DIV></b></br>' &
astrCalendar[Day(adteMonday[4])]& '</br>' &

(
If adteMonday[5] = DateAdd('M',1,{?The First Of The Required Month})
Then
        ""
Else If adteMonday[5] > (DateAdd('M',1,{?The First Of The Required
Month})+(7-DayOfWeek(DateAdd('M',1,{?The First Of The Required
Month}),crMonday))) Then
        ""
Else If adteMonday[5] > DateAdd('M',1,{?The First Of The Required
Month}) - 1 Then
        '<b><DIV ALIGN = "CENTER"> ' &
        ToText(Day(adteMonday[5]),0,'') & '</DIV></b></br>' &
        ReplicateString('</br>' , {@frmPadElements})
Else
        '<b><DIV ALIGN = "CENTER"> ' &
        ToText(Day(adteMonday[5]),0,'') & '</DIV></b></br>' &
        astrCalendar[Day(adteMonday[5])]& '</br>';)&

(
```

```
If adteMonday[6] = DateAdd('M',1,{?The First Of The Required Month})
Then
        ""
Else If adteMonday[6] > (DateAdd('M',1,{?The First Of The Required
Month})+(7-DayOfWeek(DateAdd('M',1,{?The First Of The Required
Month}),crMonday))) Then
        ""
Else If adteMonday[6] > DateAdd('M',1,{?The First Of The Required
Month}) - 1 Then
        '<b><DIV ALIGN = "CENTER"> ' &
        ToText(Day(adteMonday[6]),0,'') & '</DIV></b></br>' &
        ReplicateString('</br>' , {@frmPadElements})
Else
        '<b><DIV ALIGN = "CENTER"> ' &
        ToText(Day(adteMonday[6]),0,'') & '</DIV></b></br>' &
        astrCalendar[Day(adteMonday[6])]& '</br>';);


Code for frmTuesday in the format the report into a calendar style grid
section:

EvaluateAfter ({@frmPadElements});
Global stringVar array astrCalendar;

Local dateVar x := (
If DayOfWeek({?The First Of The Required Month},crMonday) = 2
Then
        {?The First Of The Required Month}
Else If DayOfWeek({?The First Of The Required Month},crMonday) < 2
Then
        {?The First Of The Required Month} - DayOfWeek({?The First
        Of The Required Month},crWednesday)+7
Else
        {?The First Of The Required Month} - DayOfWeek({?The First
        Of The Required Month},crWednesday));

Local dateVar array adteTuesday := [x, x+7, x+14, x+21, x+28, x+35];
```

```
'<b><DIV ALIGN = "CENTER"> ' & ToText(Day(adteTuesday[1]),0,'') &
'</DIV></b></br>' &

(If Day(adteTuesday[1])< 7 Then
        astrCalendar[Day(adteTuesday[1])]& '</br>'
Else
        ReplicateString('</br>', {@frmPadElements}))&

'<b><DIV ALIGN = "CENTER"> ' & ToText(Day(adteTuesday[2]),0,'') &
'</DIV></b></br>' &
astrCalendar[Day(adteTuesday[2])]& '</br>' &

'<b><DIV ALIGN = "CENTER"> ' & ToText(Day(adteTuesday[3]),0,'') &
'</DIV></b></br>' &
astrCalendar[Day(adteTuesday[3])]& '</br>' &

'<b><DIV ALIGN = "CENTER"> ' & ToText(Day(adteTuesday[4]),0,'') &
'</DIV></b></br>' &
astrCalendar[Day(adteTuesday[4])]& '</br>' &

(If adteTuesday[5] = DateAdd('M',1,{?The First Of The Required
Month})+1 Then
        ""
Else If adteTuesday[5] > (DateAdd('M',1,{?The First Of The Required
Month})+(7-DayOfWeek(DateAdd('M',1,{?The First Of The Required
Month}),crMonday))) Then
        ""
Else If adteTuesday[5] > DateAdd('M',1,{?The First Of The Required
Month}) - 1 Then
        '<b><DIV ALIGN = "CENTER"> ' &
        ToText(Day(adteTuesday[5]),0,'') & '</DIV></b></br>' &
        ReplicateString('</br>', {@frmPadElements})
Else
        '<b><DIV ALIGN = "CENTER"> ' &
        ToText(Day(adteTuesday[5]),0,'') & '</DIV></b></br>' &
        astrCalendar[Day(adteTuesday[5])]& '</br>';)&
```

```
(If adteTuesday[6] = DateAdd('M',1,{?The First Of The Required
Month})+1 Then
        ""

Else If adteTuesday[6] > (DateAdd('M',1,{?The First Of The Required
Month})+(7-DayOfWeek(DateAdd('M',1,{?The First Of The Required
Month}),crMonday))) Then
        ""

Else If adteTuesday[6] > DateAdd('M',1,{?The First Of The Required
Month}) - 1 Then
        '<b><DIV ALIGN = "CENTER"> ' &
        ToText(Day(adteTuesday[6]),0,'') & '</DIV></b></br>' &
        ReplicateString('</br>', {@frmPadElements})
Else
        '<b><DIV ALIGN = "CENTER"> ' &
        ToText(Day(adteTuesday[6]),0,'') & '</DIV></b></br>' &
        astrCalendar[Day(adteTuesday[6])]& '</br>';);
```

Code for frmWednesday in the format the report into a calendar style grid section:

```
EvaluateAfter ({@frmPadElements});
Global stringVar array astrCalendar;

Local dateVar x := (
If DayOfWeek({?The First Of The Required Month},crMonday) = 3
Then
        {?The First Of The Required Month}
Else If DayOfWeek({?The First Of The Required Month},crMonday) < 3
Then
        {?The First Of The Required Month} - DayOfWeek({?The First
        Of The Required Month},crThursday)+7
Else
        {?The First Of The Required Month} - DayOfWeek({?The First
        Of The Required Month},crThursday));

Local dateVar array adteWednesday := [x, x+7, x+14, x+21, x+28,
x+35];
```

```
'<b><DIV ALIGN = "CENTER"> ' &
ToText(Day(adteWednesday[1]),0,'') & '</DIV></b></br>' &

(If Day(adteWednesday[1])< 7 Then
        astrCalendar[Day(adteWednesday[1])] & '</br>'
Else
        ReplicateString('</br>', {@frmPadElements}) )&

'<b><DIV ALIGN = "CENTER"> ' &
ToText(Day(adteWednesday[2]),0,'') & '</DIV></b></br>' &
astrCalendar[Day(adteWednesday[2])]& '</br>' &

'<b><DIV ALIGN = "CENTER"> ' &
ToText(Day(adteWednesday[3]),0,'') & '</DIV></b></br>' &
astrCalendar[Day(adteWednesday[3])]& '</br>' &

'<b><DIV ALIGN = "CENTER"> ' &
ToText(Day(adteWednesday[4]),0,'') & '</DIV></b></br>' &
astrCalendar[Day(adteWednesday[4])]& '</br>' &


(If adteWednesday[5] = DateAdd('M',1,{?The First Of The Required
Month})+2 Then
        ''
Else If adteWednesday[5] > (DateAdd('M',1,{?The First Of The
Required Month})+(7-DayOfWeek(DateAdd('M',1,{?The First Of The
Required Month}),crMonday))) Then
        ''
Else If adteWednesday[5] > DateAdd('M',1,{?The First Of The Required
Month}) - 1 Then
        '<b><DIV ALIGN = "CENTER"> ' &
        ToText(Day(adteWednesday[5]),0,'') & '</DIV></b></br>' &
        ReplicateString('</br>', {@frmPadElements})
Else
        '<b><DIV ALIGN = "CENTER"> ' &
        ToText(Day(adteWednesday[5]),0,'') & '</DIV></b></br>' &
        astrCalendar[Day(adteWednesday[5])]& '</br>';)&
```

```
(If adteWednesday[6] = DateAdd('M',1,{?The First Of The Required
Month})+2 Then
        ""
Else If adteWednesday[6] > (DateAdd('M',1,{?The First Of The
Required Month})+(7-DayOfWeek(DateAdd('M',1,{?The First Of The
Required Month}),crMonday))) Then
        ""
Else If adteWednesday[6] > DateAdd('M',1,{?The First Of The Required
Month}) - 1 Then
        '<b><DIV ALIGN = "CENTER"> ' &
        ToText(Day(adteWednesday[6]),0,'') & '</DIV></b></br>' &
        ReplicateString('</br>', {@frmPadElements})
Else
        '<b><DIV ALIGN = "CENTER"> ' &
        ToText(Day(adteWednesday[6]),0,'') & '</DIV></b></br>' &
        astrCalendar[Day(adteWednesday[6])]& '</br>';);
```

Code for frmThursday in the format the report into a calendar style grid
section:

```
EvaluateAfter ({@frmPadElements});
Global stringVar array astrCalendar;

Local dateVar x := (
If DayOfWeek({?The First Of The Required Month},crMonday) = 4
Then
        {?The First Of The Required Month}
Else If DayOfWeek({?The First Of The Required Month},crMonday) < 4
Then
        {?The First Of The Required Month} - DayOfWeek({?The First
        Of The Required Month},crFriday)+7
Else
        {?The First Of The Required Month} - DayOfWeek({?The First
        Of The Required Month},crFriday));

Local dateVar array adteThursday := [x, x+7, x+14, x+21, x+28, x+35];
```

```
'<b><DIV ALIGN = "CENTER"> ' & ToText(Day(adteThursday[1]),0,'') &
'</DIV></b></br>' &

(If Day(adteThursday[1])< 7 Then
        astrCalendar[Day(adteThursday[1])] & '</br>'
Else
        ReplicateString('</br>', {@frmPadElements}))&

        '<b><DIV ALIGN = "CENTER"> ' &
        ToText(Day(adteThursday[2]),0,'') & '</DIV></b></br>' &
        astrCalendar[Day(adteThursday[2])]& '</br>' &
        '<b><DIV ALIGN = "CENTER"> ' &
        ToText(Day(adteThursday[3]),0,'') & '</DIV></b></br>' &
        astrCalendar[Day(adteThursday[3])]& '</br>' &
        '<b><DIV ALIGN = "CENTER"> ' &
        ToText(Day(adteThursday[4]),0,'') & '</DIV></b></br>' &
        astrCalendar[Day(adteThursday[4])]& '</br>' &

(If adteThursday[5] = DateAdd('M',1,{?The First Of The Required
Month})+3 Then
        ""

Else If adteThursday[5] > (DateAdd('M',1,{?The First Of The Required
Month})+(7-DayOfWeek(DateAdd('M',1,{?The First Of The Required
Month}),crMonday))) Then
        ""

Else If adteThursday[5] > DateAdd('M',1,{?The First Of The Required
Month}) - 1 Then
        '<b><DIV ALIGN = "CENTER"> ' &
        ToText(Day(adteThursday[5]),0,'') & '</DIV></b></br>' &
        ReplicateString('</br>', {@frmPadElements})
Else
        '<b><DIV ALIGN = "CENTER"> ' &
        ToText(Day(adteThursday[5]),0,'') & '</DIV></b></br>' &
        astrCalendar[Day(adteThursday[5])]& '</br>';)&

(If adteThursday[6] = DateAdd('M',1,{?The First Of The Required
Month})+3 Then
        ""
```

```
Else If adteThursday[6] > (DateAdd('M',1,{?The First Of The Required
Month})+(7-DayOfWeek(DateAdd('M',1,{?The First Of The Required
Month}),crMonday))) Then
        ""
Else If adteThursday[6] > DateAdd('M',1,{?The First Of The Required
Month}) - 1 Then
        '<b><DIV ALIGN = "CENTER"> ' &
        ToText(Day(adteThursday[6]),0,'') & '</DIV></b></br>' &
        ReplicateString('</br>', {@frmPadElements})
Else
        '<b><DIV ALIGN = "CENTER"> ' &
        ToText(Day(adteThursday[6]),0,'') & '</DIV></b></br>' &
        astrCalendar[Day(adteThursday[6])]& '</br>';);
```

Code for frmFriday in the format the report into a calendar style grid
section:

```
EvaluateAfter ({@frmPadElements});
Global stringVar array astrCalendar;

Local dateVar x := (
If DayOfWeek({?The First Of The Required Month},crMonday) = 5
Then
        {?The First Of The Required Month}
Else If DayOfWeek({?The First Of The Required Month},crMonday) < 5
Then
        {?The First Of The Required Month} - DayOfWeek({?The First
        Of The Required Month},crSaturday)+7
Else
        {?The First Of The Required Month} - DayOfWeek({?The First
        Of The Required Month},crSaturday));

Local dateVar array adteFriday := [x, x+7, x+14, x+21, x+28, x+35];

'<b><DIV ALIGN = "CENTER"> ' & ToText(Day(adteFriday[1]),0,'') &
'</DIV></b></br>' &
(If Day(adteFriday[1])< 7 Then
        astrCalendar[Day(adteFriday[1])]& '</br>'
```

```
Else
        ReplicateString('</br>', {@frmPadElements}) )&

        '<b><DIV ALIGN = "CENTER"> ' &
        ToText(Day(adteFriday[2]),0,'') & '</DIV></b></br>' &
        astrCalendar[Day(adteFriday[2])]& '</br>' &
        '<b><DIV ALIGN = "CENTER"> ' &
        ToText(Day(adteFriday[3]),0,'') & '</DIV></b></br>' &
        astrCalendar[Day(adteFriday[3])]& '</br>' &

        '<b><DIV ALIGN = "CENTER"> ' &
        ToText(Day(adteFriday[4]),0,'') & '</DIV></b></br>' &
        astrCalendar[Day(adteFriday[4])]& '</br>' &

(If adteFriday[5] = DateAdd('M',1,{?The First Of The Required
Month})+4 Then
        ""

Else If adteFriday[5] > (DateAdd('M',1,{?The First Of The Required
Month})+(7-DayOfWeek(DateAdd('M',1,{?The First Of The Required
Month}),crMonday))) Then
        ""

Else If adteFriday[5] > DateAdd('M',1,{?The First Of The Required
Month}) - 1 Then
        '<b><DIV ALIGN = "CENTER"> ' &
        ToText(Day(adteFriday[5]),0,'') & '</DIV></b></br>' &
        ReplicateString('</br>', {@frmPadElements})
Else
        '<b><DIV ALIGN = "CENTER"> ' &
        ToText(Day(adteFriday[5]),0,'') & '</DIV></b></br>' &
        astrCalendar[Day(adteFriday[5])]& '</br>';)&

(If adteFriday[6] = DateAdd('M',1,{?The First Of The Required
Month})+4 Then
        ""

Else If adteFriday[6] > (DateAdd('M',1,{?The First Of The Required
Month})+(7-DayOfWeek(DateAdd('M',1,{?The First Of The Required
Month}),crMonday))) Then
        ""
```

```
Else If adteFriday[6] > DateAdd('M',1,{?The First Of The Required
Month}) - 1 Then
        '<b><DIV ALIGN = "CENTER"> ' &
        ToText(Day(adteFriday[6]),0,'') & '</DIV></b></br>' &
        ReplicateString('</br>', {@frmPadElements})
Else
        '<b><DIV ALIGN = "CENTER"> ' &
        ToText(Day(adteFriday[6]),0,'') & '</DIV></b></br>' &
        astrCalendar[Day(adteFriday[6])]& '</br>';);
```

Code for frmSaturday in the format the report into a calendar style grid
section:

```
EvaluateAfter ({@frmPadElements});
Global stringVar array astrCalendar;

Local dateVar x := (
If DayOfWeek({?The First Of The Required Month},crMonday) = 6
Then
        {?The First Of The Required Month}
Else If DayOfWeek({?The First Of The Required Month},crMonday) < 6
Then
        {?The First Of The Required Month} - DayOfWeek({?The First
        Of The Required Month},crSunday)+7
Else
        {?The First Of The Required Month} - DayOfWeek({?The First
        Of The Required Month},crSunday));

Local dateVar array adteSaturday := [x, x+7, x+14, x+21, x+28, x+35];

'<b><DIV ALIGN = "CENTER"> ' & ToText(Day(adteSaturday[1]),0,'') &
'</DIV></b></br>' &
(If Day(adteSaturday[1])< 7 Then
        astrCalendar[Day(adteSaturday[1])]& '</br>'
Else
        ReplicateString('</br>', {@frmPadElements}))&
```

```
        '<b><DIV ALIGN = "CENTER"> ' &
        ToText(Day(adteSaturday[2]),0,'') & '</DIV></b></br>' &
        astrCalendar[Day(adteSaturday[2])]& '</br>' &

        '<b><DIV ALIGN = "CENTER"> ' &
        ToText(Day(adteSaturday[3]),0,'') & '</DIV></b></br>' &
        astrCalendar[Day(adteSaturday[3])]& '</br>' &

        '<b><DIV ALIGN = "CENTER"> ' &
        ToText(Day(adteSaturday[4]),0,'') & '</DIV></b></br>' &
        astrCalendar[Day(adteSaturday[4])]& '</br>' &

(If adteSaturday[5] = DateAdd('M',1,{?The First Of The Required
Month})+5 Then
        ""

Else If adteSaturday[5] > (DateAdd('M',1,{?The First Of The Required
Month})+(7-DayOfWeek(DateAdd('M',1,{?The First Of The Required
Month}),crMonday))) Then
        ""

Else If adteSaturday[5] > DateAdd('M',1,{?The First Of The Required
Month}) - 1 Then
        '<b><DIV ALIGN = "CENTER"> ' &
        ToText(Day(adteSaturday[5]),0,'') & '</DIV></b></br>' &
        ReplicateString('</br>', {@frmPadElements})
Else
        '<b><DIV ALIGN = "CENTER"> ' &
        ToText(Day(adteSaturday[5]),0,'') & '</DIV></b></br>' &
        astrCalendar[Day(adteSaturday[5])]& '</br>';)&

(If adteSaturday[6] = DateAdd('M',1,{?The First Of The Required
Month})+5 Then
        ""

Else If adteSaturday[6] > (DateAdd('M',1,{?The First Of The Required
Month})+(7-DayOfWeek(DateAdd('M',1,{?The First Of The Required
Month}),crMonday))) Then
        ""

Else If adteSaturday[6] > DateAdd('M',1,{?The First Of The Required
Month}) - 1 Then
```

```
        '<b><DIV ALIGN = "CENTER"> ' &
        ToText(Day(adteSaturday[6]),0,'') & '</DIV></b></br>' &
        ReplicateString('</br>', {@frmPadElements})
Else
        '<b><DIV ALIGN = "CENTER"> ' &
        ToText(Day(adteSaturday[6]),0,'') & '</DIV></b></br>' &
        astrCalendar[Day(adteSaturday[6])]& '</br>';);
```

Code for frmSunday in the format the report into a calendar style grid
section:

```
EvaluateAfter ({@frmPadElements});
Global stringVar array astrCalendar;

Local dateVar x := (
If DayOfWeek({?The First Of The Required Month},crMonday) = 7
Then
        {?The First Of The Required Month}
Else If DayOfWeek({?The First Of The Required Month},crMonday) < 7
Then
        {?The First Of The Required Month} - DayOfWeek({?The First
        Of The Required Month},crSunday)+8
Else
        {?The First Of The Required Month} - DayOfWeek({?The First
        Of The Required Month},crSunday)+1);

Local dateVar array adteSunday := [x, x+7, x+14, x+21, x+28, x+35];

'<b><DIV ALIGN = "CENTER"> ' & ToText(Day(adteSunday[1]),0,'') &
'</DIV></b></br>' &
(If Day(adteSunday[1])< 7 Then
        astrCalendar[Day(adteSunday[1])] & '</br>' Else
        ReplicateString('</br>', {@frmPadElements}) )&

'<b><DIV ALIGN = "CENTER"> ' & ToText(Day(adteSunday[2]),0,'') &
'</DIV></b></br>' &
astrCalendar[Day(adteSunday[2])]& '</br>' &
```

```
'<b><DIV ALIGN = "CENTER"> ' & ToText(Day(adteSunday[3]),0,'') &
'</DIV></b></br>' &
astrCalendar[Day(adteSunday[3])]& '</br>' &

'<b><DIV ALIGN = "CENTER"> ' & ToText(Day(adteSunday[4]),0,'') &
'</DIV></b></br>' &
astrCalendar[Day(adteSunday[4])]& '</br>' &

(If adteSunday[5] = DateAdd('M',1,{?The First Of The Required
Month})+6 Then
        ""
Else If adteSunday[5] > (DateAdd('M',1,{?The First Of The Required
Month})+(7-DayOfWeek(DateAdd('M',1,{?The First Of The Required
Month}),crMonday))) Then
        ""
Else If adteSunday[5] > DateAdd('M',1,{?The First Of The Required
Month}) - 1 Then
        '<b><DIV ALIGN = "CENTER"> ' &
        ToText(Day(adteSunday[5]),0,'') & '</DIV></b></br>' &
        ReplicateString('</br>', {@frmPadElements})
Else
        '<b><DIV ALIGN = "CENTER"> ' &
        ToText(Day(adteSunday[5]),0,'') & '</DIV></b></br>' &
        astrCalendar[Day(adteSunday[5])]& '</br>';)&

(If adteSunday[6] = DateAdd('M',1,{?The First Of The Required
Month})+6 Then
        ""
Else If adteSunday[6] > (DateAdd('M',1,{?The First Of The Required
Month})+(7-DayOfWeek(DateAdd('M',1,{?The First Of The Required
Month}),crMonday))) Then
        ""
Else If adteSunday[6] > DateAdd('M',1,{?The First Of The Required
Month}) - 1 Then
        '<b><DIV ALIGN = "CENTER"> ' &
        ToText(Day(adteSunday[6]),0,'') & '</DIV></b></br>' &
        ReplicateString('</br>', {@frmPadElements})
Else
```

```
'<b><DIV ALIGN = "CENTER"> ' &
ToText(Day(adteSunday[6]),0,'') & '</DIV></b></br>' &
astrCalendar[Day(adteSunday[6])]& '</br>';);
```

Still having problems?

The experts at Scry are here to help.

With decades of industry experience in all matters pertaining to BI, these are just some of our services:

- **BI Analysis**

- **Report Development, Implementation and Distribution.**

- **Specific Technical Solutions**

- **On Going Support**

- **BI Health Check**

- **Training**

- **Advanced Presentations**

Visit the website for more details and additional Crystal Reports formula information:

WWW.SCRY-BUSINESS-INTELLIGENCE.COM